Shella, who is a mother of two children, gained a BA (Hons) degree in public policy after studying at the Solent University, Southampton. Besides writing, she enjoys walking her two dogs in the countryside and by the sea. Shella often participates in paranormal investigations and has a passion for reading about the spirit realm and unexplained phenomena.

To Elizabeth, my inspiration. Thank you for being here, for without you, I could not have written this; and to my beloved nan, Eileen Dickson, who taught me to never give up.

Shella Hewett

ELIZABETH – SPIRIT OF A CHILD

AUSTIN MACAULEY PUBLISHERS™

LONDON • CAMBRIDGE • NEW YORK • SHARJAH

A CIP catalogue record for this title is available from the British Library.

ISBN 9781528936460 (Paperback)
ISBN 9781528968713 (ePub e-book)

www.austinmacauley.com

First Published (2021)
Austin Macauley Publishers Ltd
25 Canada Square
Canary Wharf
London
E14 5LQ

Table of Contents

Synopsis

Seeing is believing, which equates to "only physical or concrete evidence is convincing."

Although she has never shown herself to me as a full-bodied apparition, she has made herself known in many other ways.

I believe. I believe in the spirit of Elizabeth.

Author's note

As a child, I could always be found with my nose in a book or putting pen to paper. I loved words, the sheer power of them. Words that turned into sentences, paragraphs, chapters, a story. I remember saying to my mum and dad, "I'm going to be an author when I grow up." At the time, I had no idea I would write about the paranormal. That's because I hadn't met her then.

A true account about sharing my life with a spirit.

Chapter 1
Home Calling

Moving in, was no different from any other house move I've made. My husband, Graham, and I and our two young children, Mia and Sam, were looking forward to the much-needed space the house would provide. Although not large in size by anyone's standards, it was a welcome relief from our previous two-up, two-down.

On Friday 28th October 2005, we hired a modest removal van and with the help of my tireless dad, did all the lifting and shifting ourselves. Our new home was built circa 1900, a typical three-bedroom mid-terrace, situated on a relatively busy road in the town of Gosport, Hampshire. Nothing out of the ordinary one might think. It required some updating but that we knew would come with time. Looking back, I'm sure we were destined to live there because of events that had occurred beforehand.

Our initial house-hunting involved viewing many properties, one of them being a house in the nearby town of Fareham. This was my hometown, the place where I grew up and spent twenty-six years of my life. Coming from a close-knit family, I was keen to move near my parents, grandparents and brother, who still live in Fareham. Naturally, I thought the most important thing was that Mia and Sam should be around them, enjoying the closeness that I had experienced as a child.

We viewed a house. It was exactly what we wanted. Although it was slightly above our price range, we made an immediate offer for the full asking price. It was accepted. Excited about the prospect of being back in Fareham, I was astonished when the estate agent telephoned with the news. Bad news. Bitterly disappointed, I learnt that the vendor had unexpectedly taken the property off the market. It was claimed that moving house would be detrimental to her health. Interestingly though, the very same house was back on the market within a week but at a much higher price. Unfortunately, it was a price we couldn't stretch to.

I suspect the real reason behind the sudden change of mind came down to one thing. Money. Despite us having agreed to pay the full price, I believe the realisation set in that she could make more. All at once, we were faced with a considerable stumbling block and we had to find a way to overcome it.

It is said that time is of the essence and that was certainly the case for us. A buyer had been lined up for our property and he desperately wanted to move in. We were under tremendous pressure to find a new home. However, as our initial choice had fallen through, we now had to find somewhere else to live. The very next day, I made a phone call and waited in anticipation for someone to answer. After what seemed like an eternity, the estate agent spoke. He greeted me in a warm and friendly manner.

Arrangements were made for us to view a house we had previously looked at. The house that was to become our new home. On both occasions it had felt homely, with a welcoming air about it. The proprietor at the time was a likeable lady, as welcoming as the house itself. She had been living in the property for twelve years and loved her home dearly, so she felt sad at the prospect of having to sell, for reasons I won't go into. At the time of the second viewing, I noticed that the adjoining house was up for sale with the same estate agents. Out of curiosity, I made an appointment to view it the following day.

Walking in, I noticed that the house let in a vast amount of light. Light then beckoned me like a full moon on a cloudless evening. Everything was immaculate. Everything was in its place. As Graham and I looked around each room, we knew it was above and beyond what we could have hoped for and at a less expensive price. There and then, we decided to make an offer for the full asking price. This was our second chance at buying a property that we were really keen on. (Apart from it not being in Fareham of course!) I couldn't let it slip through my fingers.

Anxiously, I waited for the estate agent to get back to me. Eventually, the phone rang. It was the call I'd been expecting. He went on to tell me the house had been taken off the market; it was no longer for sale. I could hardly believe what I was hearing. Surely, this couldn't be happening again, not a second time. My heart sank with disbelief. Questions raced through my mind. *Who? What? When? Where? Why? How?* Confused, I just couldn't ask them out loud. There were no answers. The estate agent apologised profusely. I couldn't believe it. The house had been up for sale and we were willing to pay the full asking price, so what was the problem? There shouldn't be a problem. Surely.

Home was calling. Although I didn't realise it at the time, it was meant to be. My family and I moved into the house, our house, our new home. Despite all that had happened beforehand, we settled in quickly. A few days after we had moved in, our next-door neighbour (whose house we'd wanted to buy) explained over the fence why she had taken her house off the market. "Oh, we had to take it off the market so you'd buy your house. She was desperate to sell because she had debts." 'She' being the proprietor.

At that moment, I felt upset, yet incensed at the same time. At least I knew the real reason behind the decision to withdraw the sale but why tell me now? What good could it do? There stood this woman so shameless and bold, who was telling me things I now didn't need to know. Talk about rubbing salt into the wound! As painful as it was to hear her words, I couldn't let her show how much they upset me. I had to hide it. I did hide it.

Surprisingly, I didn't hold it against her. It soon became water under the bridge.

I had to live next door so I wanted to maintain a good neighbourly relationship. Subsequently, we would exchange pleasantries whenever we met and things ran smoothly between us.

I cannot recall exactly when events first started to occur, certainly not when I first moved into my new home. Graham went to work, I stayed at home and the children went to school. After having both Mia and Sam, I had taken on the role of a full-time mum. Days, then weeks passed. Although I spent a great deal of time in the house, I didn't sense anything out of the ordinary.

A short time later, (which I recall being winter time) the first of many unusual occurrences took place. It was a vision. Graham had kept his thoughts of the initial sighting to himself because he didn't want me to feel panicked by what he had witnessed. It was only when he observed these sightings on a more frequent basis, he hesitantly decided to confide in me.

Cautiously, Graham went on to explain about the visions. A dog. They were visions of a dog! To his eyes, it would present itself as a solid form and appeared no less real than a living canine. I went on to learn, it had been seen in various locations throughout the house. According to Graham, this spirit dog was medium-sized with a short, golden coat and it resembled a Labrador retriever. It appeared to be peaceful and content, as if it belonged with us.

Fortunately, there was nothing menacing about the spirit dog in any shape or form. Often, Graham would see it resting in front of our living room fire, as if keeping itself warm. Astonishingly, it was also seen lying beside a radiator, (which was turned on at the time) as if appreciating the heat that was being emitted. Strangely though, the base of the radiator felt unusually cold when the spirit dog was there.

On one occasion, I was washing-up in the kitchen when a rubber ball, which belonged to my children, came rolling into the room and stopped exactly where I was standing. As it happened, Mia and Sam were playing elsewhere in the house, and Graham had watched the ball move. Phenomenally, it bounced across the length of the lounge, hit the end wall, bounced back and proceeded to roll to where I was in the kitchen. Due to the strange angle and the distance it had travelled, we believe the spirit dog had been playing chase with the ball. Although Graham had not seen the spirit dog at that precise time, he had seen it downstairs many times leading up to this event.

There's that dreadful smell when a dog's been out in the rain, that horrible, wet dog smell. It was late one evening, while Graham and I were watching television, when the distinct odour engulfed us. All of a sudden, I noticed that my right thigh became as cold as ice yet, the rest of my leg remained warm to the touch. Feeling nervous, I didn't know what to do. As this occurred, Graham's gaze fell upon a translucent but definite image of a dog. The spirit dog. Its head was resting on my thigh and this appeared to be the cause of my coldness. A few minutes passed, before the warmth returned to my thigh. The spirit dog had vanished! It was a breath-taking moment and I felt moved by the encounter.

Soon after this occurrence, it was Christmas time and my parents, along with my nan, came to visit me. Everyone felt relaxed and happy and there was a friendly, warm atmosphere in the house. At one point, Mum excused herself to use the bathroom and left the room, making her way upstairs. As she approached the landing, something caught her eye. Hesitantly, she took a closer look and what she saw made her heart race. Resting next to my bedroom door, was the blurred outline of a dog. Remaining level-headed, Mum stood still and stared but in a blink of an eye, it disappeared. Afterwards, she announced that her eyes had not deceived her. It came as no surprise that the description she gave, resembled that of the spirit dog.

We had been storing some household items for the previous owner, just until she moved from a temporary address to her permanent home. On collection of her possessions, I mentioned that Graham had seen the spirit of a dog about the house. To be honest, it had been difficult to broach the subject of the paranormal. As luck would have it, she didn't seem shocked or surprised at what I was saying. Candidly, she told me that seeing twinkling lights at the foot of the stairs was a regular occurrence for the household. She went on to say they had never been worried by it and felt the presence was good-natured. I was relieved to know that similar phenomena had been experienced in the house before, as it gave us confirmation of what we already knew.

I also found it interesting when I got chatting about the spirit dog with my elderly neighbour. Straight away, she told me that she'd lived next door to our property for twenty-five years. Curiously, I enquired as to whether any previous residents had dogs matching the description to that of the dog Graham had seen. The conversation revealed there had been many different dogs in my home over the years but not one quite like the spirit dog. I then wondered if it had been resident here a long time ago.

Thinking back, it was difficult to understand why the spirit dog would visit my home but one thing I did know is that it was always welcome. I often thought about who had owned it. It wasn't until much later that I found the answer to my question. Elizabeth, it belonged to Elizabeth.

Chapter 2
Popping Corn

Golden-coloured popcorn danced upon the wooden floor. It captured my attention. The sound was like light rain descending on a tin roof. I couldn't believe what I had witnessed. Feeling nervous, I took a good look around. Gingerly, I gathered up the kernels from their resting place and studied them. A warmth emanated from them as though someone had been clutching them tightly. They must have come from somewhere but had appeared out of nowhere. I wanted to get to the bottom of this but didn't know where to start. Thinking long and hard, I still could not make sense of the situation.

Earlier that evening, Mia and I had been making popcorn from scratch. Carefully, we heated the saucepan adding a knob of salted butter. As soon as the butter had melted, we tossed in a handful of kernels and placed the glass lid on top. A few minutes later, the popping slowed down. Most of the kernels had burst opened. Without hesitation, we transferred the white and yellowish popcorn to a large bowl, ready to eat. Fluffy puffs of corn covered the hard, uncooked pieces that lay beneath.

After some reflection, I realised the kernels had been dropped from above, judging by the way they had bounced in all directions. It was as if they had fallen from the living room ceiling. I was perplexed. One thing I was sure of, is they weren't thrown by human hands. This is when I first questioned if there was someone else with me, someone from the spirit world.

Nervously, I called out. "Are there any spirits here with me?" The silence was deafening. I called out a second time. My words came out tentatively. "Is there anybody here?" There was no response. In a way, I felt relieved that I was alone but on my third attempt, I was astounded to hear a faint sound. It was a knock. I could only describe it like the noise a knuckle makes when striking a piece of wood. Further questions followed. "Are you a male spirit?" It remained silent. "Are you a female spirit?" This time I heard an unmistakable knock. The answer must be 'yes'.

In next to no time, I asked, "Was it you who used the popcorn to attract my attention?" Swiftly, I heard a knock, even more definite than before. To my surprise, I felt more at ease with each passing question. I soon established that one knock meant 'yes' and silence meant 'no'. Wanting to find out her first name, I began at the letter 'A' and slowly went through the alphabet. When I reached the letter 'E', she knocked to acknowledge this was correct. I then went through the same process to find out the second letter of her name, which happened to be 'L'.

From the replies received, I called out various names until I discovered I was communicating with a spirit named Elizabeth. The Elizabeth that I know and love today. As I could only get yes and no answers, I had to be careful how I worded my questions.

Continuing with the conversation, I went on to discover that she was born in the Victorian era but I couldn't ascertain an exact date of birth. What did come to light was that tuberculosis claimed her life. Elizabeth was only seven years old. I didn't expect that. Sadly, tuberculosis was rife before and around the turn of the twentieth century. I felt deeply moved that I was communicating with the spirit of a child. Thinking back to the popcorn episode, I should have guessed Elizabeth was a youngster. I'm sure she had so much fun playing with the kernels, as anyone her age would.

With ever-increasing confidence, I called out, "Did you used to live in this house?" The knock was clearly audible. It had been acknowledged that at some time in the past, my home had been her home. I wanted to find out more. Before long, I learnt that her family unit consisted of her parents and brother, Samuel. Our now upstairs bathroom was once Elizabeth's bedroom. Excitedly, I asked her if she knew who the spirit dog was and she responded with a knock. It transpired that his name was Boy and that he was her pet. I was amazed. Until now, it hadn't occurred to me that Boy had belonged to somebody in spirit. Best of all, I'd found out that they were together.

At this point, I was surprised when Elizabeth softly knocked twice. I hadn't asked a question. To be honest, I didn't know the relevance of two knocks. (I have since discovered it symbolises the end of a communication.) Regrettably, the time had come for our conversation to end. This incredible event was the first of many that I've been blessed to have.

Feeling exhausted after a marvellous day out at Fort Nelson, I put the key in my front door, glad to be home. The settee looked welcoming so I settled down, my head resting on a soft cushion. Sleep came easily. Earlier that day, I had wandered the nineteen acres of land, exploring the underground tunnels along the way.

As it happened, I slept for longer than I intended. On awakening, I felt content and refreshed. Slowly, I went to stand up, when approximately fifteen popcorn kernels plummeted to the ground. I turned around. What I saw amazed me. In addition, there were another hundred or so kernels on the settee. To say I was puzzled, was an understatement. The remarkable thing about it was the fact that I had been sleeping soundly, yet somehow a substantial number of kernels had been placed beneath me. How on earth could they have got there when I hadn't even moved? Painstakingly, I gathered them all up and put them in a breakfast bowl on the table. It was difficult to understand why this had occurred but it reinforced my newfound belief in the paranormal.

I'm one of those people that love writing lists. So, late one night, I was scribbling in my notepad, when I decided it was time for a comfort break. On my return, I picked up my notepad and from four pages in, popcorn kernels suddenly plummeted onto the settee and floor. Startled, I stood there in disbelief. I counted seventy-three kernels in total. Graham was aware that I'd been busy writing all evening, so he thought he'd ask Elizabeth a question. He called out. "Did you put the popcorn in Shella's notebook because you wanted her to stop writing?" I heard an unmistakable knock. It meant 'yes'. As it was 10:45 pm, I suppose she was right. I had been writing for several hours and had been feeling increasingly tired. The time had obviously come for me to call it a day.

I wondered what the significance was behind the seventy-three kernels. My mind was racing, I had to find out. After researching on the internet, I discovered the answer to my question. In numerology, seventy-three is a powerful spiritual number. Was there a hidden meaning? I guess I'll never really know.

On another occasion, a huge bowl of freshly cooked popcorn had been shared amongst the four of us. After we had finished eating, Graham went upstairs while Mia and Sam remained in the living room with me. It was no surprise that there was an abundance of leftover kernels. (You always get the ones that come to nothing!) Although I was about to put them in the kitchen bin, I soon stopped dead in my tracks when I heard a distinct *'tap, tap'*. It was that familiar sound: the sound of a hard kernel hitting the surface of the wooden floor. I looked around. There it went again. Another one flew through the air and meandered across the floor. It became apparent that Elizabeth wanted to get my attention. Well, she certainly had it now. Carefully, I collected the kernels one at a time and held them tightly in my right hand.

I wondered whether Elizabeth wanted to play catch. Now you can just imagine how difficult it would be to catch a speeding kernel. Gently, I threw one across the room to invisible hands. It ricocheted, then settled on the ground but what happened next astonished me. In no time at all, the same kernel came flying through the air towards me, as if she was returning my throw. Obligingly, we continued to toss the kernels back and forth to each other. It was spectacular. I asked Mia if she wanted to have a go and she immediately jumped at the chance; she was so excited. As soon as she had thrown it, another one came back at her. Her enjoyment was obvious. Meanwhile, Sam asked if he could play so Mia offered him several kernels. It was unmissable to see the glisten in his eyes and his visible smile, as he beheld the mind-blowing movement of the kernels. My head constantly turned from left to right. Funnily, it reminded me of watching table tennis when your eyes are glued to the Ping-Pong ball. Luckily, the children weren't worried by what they saw; to them, it was just a fun game. After five minutes had passed, the paranormal activity came to a grinding halt. What we had seen and participated in was truly unforgettable.

After spending the night on the settee, I woke up at 12.45 p.m. having slept through my alarm. I must have been too tired the previous evening to get myself off to bed. Sitting up with a start, I was astounded when ten kernels descended upon the wooden floor. Strangely, there were further kernels inside the soft, pink fleece that covered my warm legs. What on earth was going on? How did they even get there? I was completely baffled.

Before long, I briefly left the living room. On my return, I could only find three of the kernels that had fallen to the ground. What is clear is that I had counted ten before, there was no doubt about it. Patiently, I searched the entire area, looking on, around, above and below the furnishings. Despite the fact that I had been so thorough, I couldn't find a single kernel. They had simply vanished into thin air. My thoughts were that Elizabeth must have collected up seven of the kernels and taken them. I suppose it was just one of those things she liked to do. It couldn't be explained or understood. Wondering why she had left some behind, I tried calling out to her but there was no answer. Then my attention turned back to the settee. I could see the kernels that had been hiding inside the fleece. They rested there as still as the dead of night. The atmosphere was peaceful, except for the ticking of the old-fashioned clock. It seemed the activity stopped as quickly as it had begun.

It was late in the evening and I had finally finished all the housework that needed to be done. Even though I felt in need of sleep, I decided to call out to Elizabeth before heading upstairs to bed. Standing in the kitchen, I asked, "Elizabeth, can you give me a sign you're here, please?" There was no response, so I repeated the same words again. It remained silent. I persisted. "Can you tap or throw some popcorn, please?" Nothing happened. I thought that maybe she couldn't come through. Disappointed, I switched off the lights. The time had come for me to rest.

Sunlight streamed through the gap in the curtains. It was early the next morning, when I climbed out of my cosy bed. I leisurely got dressed and prepared for the day ahead. As I felt like listening to some music, I put my headphones on and made my way downstairs. While I glanced around the living room, I happened to notice the time was 9.28 a.m.

I was walking towards the kitchen, when I became aware of a lone kernel upon the brown, wooden table. It definitely hadn't been there the previous evening. Feeling puzzled, I wondered if I would find anymore, so I carefully searched all over the room. I was surprised when I found two kernels on the wooden floor next to the black beanbag. It then came to my attention that there was also a solitary kernel lying on the shag pile rug.

The day before, I'd asked Elizabeth for a sign that she was there. Could she have brought them forward in response to my questions? Unfortunately, I hadn't heard the kernels fall to the ground because I was wearing headphones. For all I know, Elizabeth might have even sent them at an earlier time. This was an episode I was left to wonder about.

After living in the house for several months, my nan, Eileen, and Auntie Jen came to visit for the first time. We settled down with our steaming cups of tea and had a casual and unhurried conversation. Towards nightfall, I drew the curtains and turned the lights on before showing them around the many different rooms. It was a pleasant evening and I was enjoying their company.

The time came for them to say goodbye. As Jen stood up and was about to leave, she felt as though someone had brushed across her fringe with their hand, creating a tickling sensation on her forehead. She was stunned by what she had experienced. Her belief was that she had been touched by a spirit. She was aware about Elizabeth and was certain her hair had been stroked by a child's fingers. As I was about to show Nan and Jen out the front door, we heard a noise like something had landed upon the ground. It came from the far-left hand corner of the living room. Confident I would come across something, I instantly ran to where I heard the sound and found a popcorn kernel, all by itself.

Later on, after my guests had gone, I decided to call out to Elizabeth to find out if she had been with us. I began with, "Elizabeth, were you here when my nan and Jen visited this evening?" I heard a definite knock. This meant 'yes' so I was over the moon. I then continued, "Elizabeth, did you affect Jen by touching her hair?" She knocked 'yes' in her response. I then asked, "Did you throw a popcorn kernel on the floor as Jen was leaving tonight?" Once again she knocked 'yes'. While I knew Elizabeth was here, I thought I'd put forward some additional questions. "Do you think Jen is a lovely person? Do you think Jen is a very spiritual person? Are you aware her husband, Eric, has passed over?" There was one knock in reply to each of these questions, which confirmed the answers as 'yes'. At the end of the conversation, I heard two unmistakable knocks, which meant Elizabeth was leaving.

I felt so grateful that Elizabeth had been responsive to all of my questions. This is and always will be something that I find overwhelmingly, every single time it happens. It is never taken for granted. I am always appreciative.

As I was thinking about writing this chapter, which is predominately about occurrences related to popcorn, I found a single kernel. Resting upon the floral cushion in the dog basket, it had appeared out of nowhere. Was it a sign? I could only think it was Elizabeth, giving me the go-ahead to continue to tell her story.

Chapter 3
Round and Around

It's a little bigger than a fifty pence piece. Plastic and hexagonal in shape, it is coloured gloss black. The gleaming, silver spindle stands proudly in the centre. A simple twist of the fingers and twirl of the wrist makes it come alive. This spinner has been the focus of many paranormal occurrences.

Shoe shopping for children is never easy so I bought Sam's from a well-known footwear retailer. They made the experience as painless as possible, with the additional incentive of selling shoes with a toy in the heel. What child could resist that! Sam certainly couldn't.

After trying on a number of shoes, Sam chose a navy-blue pair which came with two spinners. His whole face lit up with excitement. Full of beans, he couldn't wait to play with them. Sam was happy, I was happy; we went home.

Initially, Sam had an action-packed time playing with the spinners but it wasn't long before he lost interest in them. Sadly, his new favourite toys were forgotten and packed away in his games' cupboard. Months passed, then it began. At first, the spinners appeared in places the children said they hadn't put them. I was perplexed. Maybe they were amusing themselves with a secret and clever scheme, something they didn't want me to know about. I'm sure that wasn't the case though. I later realised they were telling the truth.

The spinners' new hidey-hole was inside a trinket box. An angel by design, Mia had hand-painted the ceramic piece at a local pottery shop. She had made a fine job of it. Kneeling on a white cushion, the angel has her hands clasped safely in her lap. Long, brown hair tumbles over her golden-coloured robe and blue wings fold neatly at her side. I keep this angelic ornament inside a glass-fronted cabinet in the living room.

A spinner. Who would have ever thought that such a simple child's toy, would be the focus of so much and so many different kinds of activity. One of the initial places I used to find the spinners would be on the wooden staircase posts. I have a first flight of stairs leading off to the landing, then two bedrooms and a family bathroom. In addition, there is a second flight of narrow stairs leading up to an attic bedroom.

Opening the living room door to the foot of the stairs, I reached out to put my left hand on the banister and it was then that I caught sight of the spinner, resting upon that first post. When I reached the top of the stairs, the other spinner had appeared on the second post. Heading downstairs, I discovered that both of them had vanished. This happened often. On other occasions, I would find one on the lower post of the attic stairs.

Every now and then, one spinner would be on the first post and then in the time it had taken me to walk up the stairs it was already waiting for me on the second post. Steadfast, the other spinner would still be inside the trinket box. Sometimes they stayed, other times they didn't. Amazingly, the spinners would either disappear for a considerable amount of time or show up straight away on a different post. It's always made me wonder where they go during that intervening time. What is clear, is that Elizabeth loves playing with the spinners. Mostly, they were laid flat and only every so often were they set with the spindle upright, as if primed to spin. Even though such events have occurred countless times, it never ceases to amaze me.

There have been a couple of strange incidents relating to the spinners and this book. One lunchtime, I had been talking to Graham about them and I had the urge to check they were still inside the angel trinket box. My conversation had turned to the spinners because later that day, I was about to start writing this chapter. In the evening, I picked up my manuscript, about to write, when a spinner fell from its plastic folder onto the wooden floor. I was stunned.

Three days later, Graham and I were in the living room, when we thought we heard the sound of a spinner landing on the kitchen floor. Funnily, the noise resembled a can of drink being opened. Even though we searched thoroughly, there was nothing there. A few moments passed, then I heard the same sound in the living room and on this occasion, I found a spinner on the wooden floor next to the dinner table. I put it back where it belonged with the other spinner.

An hour later, I was still in the living room when I heard the same noise again but this time on the kitchen floor. I found the spinner, picked it up and went to put it away, when once again the other one landed on the wooden floor next to the dinner table. My dog, Baya, heard it and she looked exactly where it had landed. The spinners were put away. Not long afterwards, I checked the spinners were still safely in the angel trinket box. They were. I went upstairs, came down again and in the two minutes that I was gone, they had disappeared. Two little minutes; I was astonished. It wasn't until the following morning that I noticed both the spinners on top of each other underneath the three-seater settee. They were tucked about ten centimetres in from the edge. I couldn't believe it. Picking them up, I placed them back where they belonged.

Being inactive for some time before the last two events took place, it seems odd that the spinners suddenly became the focus of activity. Was it Elizabeth encouraging me to pursue my writing? I'm sure it was. It seemed strange that the timing had coincided with me writing about spinners.

Still feeling exhausted after a long night's sleep, I made my way downstairs to the living room. I'm not exactly sure why but I had a strong desire to check the two spinners were in their usual place. I looked. It soon became apparent they were missing. Glancing around the room, I was hoping to catch sight of them but to no avail. Fifteen minutes passed and it was then that I spotted a spinner, quite by accident.

Remarkably, it was balanced on top of the head of a ballerina ornament. This sat one shelf above the angel trinket box.

I have recurrent depressive disorder and I was feeling particularly despondent. As the spinner had been placed on the ballerina's head, I wonder whether it was representing and referring to my frame of mind at that time. When I talked to Mia about this, she thought it meant balance. The balance of the mind. Could this have been a message from Elizabeth? Was she looking out for me? What I do know, is that the spinner had not been there the first time I looked around.

Despite the fact that I had been very careful cleaning my Syrian hamster's cage out, I still managed to get fresh sawdust all over the living room floor. When it was time to tidy up, out came the cylinder vacuum cleaner. Hurriedly, I vacuumed the shag pile rug which seemed to take an eternity. The sawdust was so deeply embedded, it was difficult to remove. At one point, I accidentally pulled the lead too far and it immediately stopped working. This is when I found out the plug had come part way out the electric socket. I went over to push the plug back in when I noticed that a spinner was lying on top of the vacuum cleaner. Prior to this, I had vacuumed under the stairs where it had been pulled around and even turned on its side. If the spinner had been on it then, it would most definitely had fallen off. Incredibly, in the space of five minutes, the spinner had been placed on the vacuum cleaner.

At another time, while standing in the living room, Graham became aware of an orb of hazy, pale light. Staggered, he paid particular attention to how it moved, describing it as rapid and making an arc. He likened it to how we see the shape of a fully-formed rainbow. Its starting point was from where the spinners were kept in the angel trinket box, reaching about four feet across to where I usually sit on the three-seater settee. Quickly, Graham called me over and it was then that I discovered one of the spinners was missing from its place. I only checked because this is where he first saw the orb. Then I noticed it, lying upon my mobile phone. This was resting on the right arm of the three-seater settee, the finishing point of the orb movement. It was a mind-blowing moment for both of us.

It was late in the evening and I was watching television in the living room. Graham and I cracked open a can of cold lager and relaxed. I set down my drink on the little table next to me, which was within easy reach. After chatting for a while, I picked up my can to take a sip. This is when I noticed that there was a spinner underneath, laying on the table. I didn't expect that! It wasn't there before. Then I went to look in the angel trinket box and noticed that both the spinners were missing. Strangely, the other one was sat on the cabinet shelf in front of my guardian angel ornament. I was utterly astonished.

On another occasion, I was sitting on the two-seater settee and when I stood up, I noticed a large, orange bouncy ball was on the settee next to where I had sat. Confused, I had no idea where it had come from. Cautiously, I made my way to the kitchen and a smaller, orange bouncy ball rolled in towards me. It knocked me for six. Minutes earlier, I had picked up my can of lager from the black coffee table and found that one of the spinners was underneath. I put it back in the angel trinket box.

Fifteen minutes passed and I picked up my can of lager from the same place and found that the other spinner was underneath it. I put this one back so both of them were in their rightful place. An hour passed and the spinners disappeared again. I checked under the can. Nothing was there. At this point, I went to take my make-up off upstairs and then came back down to continue chatting to Graham. Taking a sip of my drink, I found a spinner underneath it. I was amazed. Straight away, I put it back in the angel trinket box. Then I went to get Graham a drink from the kitchen and I had this strong feeling that the spinner would be under my can again when I returned. It was. I put it back where it belonged. This was an incredible experience. Perhaps,

Elizabeth has an aversion to alcoholic beverages. It certainly seems that way.

Often, I would find the spinner inside my brown, leather handbag. It was the one I always took to work. On the first occasion, I picked up my bag and found the spinner was tucked inside the outside pocket. I couldn't believe my eyes. It went missing the day before so it could have been there since then. I decided to put it back inside the angel trinket box. When I opened it, I noticed the other spinner was still there.

It was a Saturday afternoon and I was about to go shopping. I went to check how much money I had in my purse and when I opened it, the spinner was there mingled with the coins. I was completely taken aback. Was Elizabeth trying to tell me something, or was she simply having fun? It was a unique experience because it never happened again.

One morning, I was in the bathroom about to clean my glasses before wearing them. It was part of my usual daily routine. I opened the black case and went to pick up the lens cloth when I discovered a spinner underneath it. Then I called down to Mia who was in the living room and asked if she could see how many spinners were in the angel trinket box. Shortly afterwards, Mia shouted up that both spinners had gone. I wondered where the other one was. It hadn't shown up in the same place.

It was no surprise that I found my adorable cat, Ginger, sleeping in the living room. He looked majestic like a lion, laying upon the pink fleece on the three-seater settee. I went over to stroke him and he stretched out as he enjoyed the attention. A couple of minutes passed before he stood up and casually slinked to the floor. Picking up the fleece, I uncovered my magazine. This is when I set eyes on a spinner lying upon it. Seconds later, I picked the magazine up to put it away and the spinner went flying across the room. It reached the two-seater settee, which was some distance away. That came as a bit of a surprise.

On a further occasion, Graham was clearing out the rickety wardrobes in our bedroom. They desperately needed replacing, so he was careful as he sifted through them. Next to the wardrobe, resting on its stand, was a particular guitar which was of great sentimental value to me. I say this because it had belonged to my granddad before he passed away. It was one of three guitars that I occasionally enjoyed playing. Moving it out of the way, Graham suddenly heard a rattling noise from inside the body of the guitar. Gently, he tipped and gently shook it. Simultaneously, something small fell to the carpet below. He had thought something was broken inside the guitar. On closer inspection, Graham recognised it was a spinner. We had noticed that one was missing from its usual place, but it was normally situated where I would find it. This time it wasn't the case. Funnily enough, Mia played the same guitar after school the next evening and she would have been the one to find the spinner. I probably wouldn't have moved the guitar so maybe Graham was meant to find it that time.

The first time it happened, I was about to walk into the living room through the white painted door at the bottom of the stairs. As I opened the door, I saw something come hurtling down in front of me. It bounced across the wooden floor like a stone that skims the water. Then lo and behold, what should I see sitting on the ground but the spinner. Strangely, it appeared to have come from above the door. Out of sheer curiosity, I closed the door and attempted to place the spinner on top. It wasn't possible. The gap between the top and the frame was nowhere near wide enough.

This also became apparent with the porch door which opened to the living room. I'd come into the house and on opening the door, something would whoosh past me. After hearing a rat-a-tat-tat, it would then become silent. On looking around, the spinner would be there, settled on the wooden floor. Maybe it had come from higher up but it seemed to have come from the top of the door. It was like it was balanced, waiting for me to pull down the handle. Furthermore, it always happened to me rather than Graham, Mia or Sam.

These occurrences were frequent and I half expected that a spinner would fall down in front of me whenever I opened one of the doors. For that reason, it soon became the norm. It did make me jump on occasions but I never felt afraid. I knew it was Elizabeth trying to get my attention.

I have canvas pictures of flowers to brighten up my living room, lots of reds, whites and a little green and blue. Often I would sit there and lose myself in them. It wasn't long before the spinners became apparent, perched on top of the pictures. Usually I would notice one or both of them when I walked into the room. Sometimes they were up high, other times at eye level. They appeared regularly and I wondered if Elizabeth was giving her seal of approval to the different flowers. Occasionally, the spinners would disappear from one picture only to reappear on another. Soon, I became so used to seeing the spinners that I would look for them every time I set foot in the living room.

Other experiences I've had involve the use of laundry. Before long, the clothes on the two radiators were bone dry. I went to remove a couple of items from the double radiator, when I saw a spinner nestled between the fabric of a long-sleeved t-shirt. It certainly hadn't been there earlier, as I had put the washing there myself. I was astonished. This type of phenomena occurred on many occasions, most often in the living room. Elizabeth would place the spinners on various pieces of clothing, she wasn't fussed as to what it was. I'm sure what she did want and know, was that I would always be the one to find them.

I recall a time when I had a beautiful jar candle. Slowly, the sweet scent of vanilla would fill the air from a centrally placed point on the living room table. One particular time, I went to light the candle when I became aware of a spinner beside the blackened wick. Wondering what the dark shape was from a distance, I now had my answer. I gently removed the spinner and placed it back safely inside the angel trinket box. The burning of candles for spiritual purposes dates back to ancient times. Was this why Elizabeth had left the spinner there or was she simply telling me she liked the pleasant smell? Not once had this arisen before and never has since.

It was a little rubber duck, no bigger than a quail's egg. Seldom did I find it by itself, it nearly always sat on top of a spinner. Frequently, they appeared in many different locations such as the arms of the settee, the living room table and above the fire. Another favourite spot was on top of the television, as well as upon the banister posts and the shelves of the glass-fronted cabinet. Other times, I would find them both sitting on my mobile phone. Once again, they were always in places where I would notice them before anyone else in the family did. I believe that Elizabeth truly loved playing with that rubber duck and she obviously found it amusing, as she kept moving it so often. It always makes me smile when I think about it.

Rose Quartz, is a stone of the heart, a crystal of unconditional love. Consequently, it carries a soft, feminine energy that embodies the vibration of love. It is a gemstone that I have and often, I would find it on top of the spinner which would be upon my mobile phone. I'm not entirely sure why but these three objects were always together, placed in exactly the same order. I would usually see them on the arm of the settee so they captured my attention as soon as I sat down. Perhaps Elizabeth liked what this stone represented, after all she was a feminine energy herself.

Sometimes I would go to pick up my reporters notepad and see a spinner on it. Other times I would pick the notepad up and a spinner would fall to the ground below. I was staggered when it didn't always emerge instantly. It seemed to wait a number of seconds before it fell. Strangely, it was as if something or someone was holding it in place before suddenly releasing it. What is clear is that it was spectacular to see.

Now and again I buy lottery tickets and on several occasions I discovered the spinner resting on them. I used to hope that Elizabeth was giving me a sign that they'd be winning ones. Unfortunately, most of the time they weren't.

On the other hand, she may have been warning me not to waste my money.

Even today as I am writing this book, the activity continues. What's more, it also occurred yesterday when I called out to Elizabeth, asking if she could move the two spinners and put them on top of the canvas prints. It was mid-afternoon when I looked inside the angel trinket box and became aware the spinners had both gone missing. Without hesitation, I scanned the pictures in the living room and my eyes settled on a canvas with a spinner balanced on top of it. However, the second one was nowhere to be found. A short while later, the spinner caught my eye. It was tucked neatly behind the six strings at the bridge of my late granddad's guitar. This moved me because it was the eighth anniversary of my granddad's passing. The day before, Graham had hung the guitar on one of the walls in the living room, using a guitar bracket. Was it Elizabeth or a sign from my granddad?

Having fallen asleep on the three-seater settee, I woke up this morning to discover that my puppy, Freddie, was playing with something. I wasn't quite sure what it was until the clink, clink, clinking noise offered me a distinctive clue. That sound; it was that familiar sound. Looking closely, I uncovered a spinner. Out of curiosity, I half-blindly went to see if the second spinner had disappeared from the angel trinket box. It had. I hadn't got around to putting my glasses on at this stage, so I carefully walked back to collect them. There on the windowsill behind the settee, were my black and white glasses, and on the left arm there was the second spinner. The arm was stuck firmly through the central hole. It was an impressive sight and one that I had never encountered before.

Chapter 4
Cornish Cross

Hanging down from a sterling silver chain, is a sterling silver cross encrusted with six, oval-shaped rubies. I bought this necklace from a quaint shop in Boscastle, Cornwall, a number of years ago. I'm not really one for jewellery but on this occasion, I'd felt drawn to buying the necklace. Funnily enough, I'd always had my heart set on a cross. I wear it every day so it almost feels like a part of me.

After wearing my necklace until the evening, I always put it away in my bedroom draw for safekeeping. As I don't own a jewellery box, it's the next best thing. Often, the necklace would disappear overnight. One morning, I went to put my necklace on ready for work, only to find it was missing. I rummaged around but it was nowhere to be seen. It was about forty-five minutes later when I opened the drawer again. Astonishingly, the necklace was where it should have been in the first place. That very same day after work, I placed my necklace in the drawer as usual. When I opened it later that evening, the necklace had vanished into thin air. I wonder if Elizabeth is drawn to the necklace because it is so personal to me.

Following a hard day at work, I put my necklace away in the bedroom drawer as usual. As it had disappeared twice the day before, I was eager to check the drawer a little later on to see if it was still there. When I did, I discovered the necklace was gone. To be honest, I knew it would turn up somewhere where I would easily see it. I was happily scribbling in my notepad, when something caught my eye. Being some distance away, I couldn't quite make it out at first but when I looked to my right-hand side, I noticed that my necklace was inside the unlit jar candle on the living room table. The glass lid was still on. Gently, I removed the lid and carefully took it out. It smelt exquisite, with the subtle scent of vanilla. I wondered how Elizabeth had moved the necklace to the jar in the first place. Had she removed and replaced the lid or had it been transported through the glass? This type of phenomena was absolutely incredible.

More activity happened early one morning, when I began to draw my heavy bedroom curtains open. As I did, my necklace came flying down from above and struck my right hand before landing on the soft carpet. Thankfully, my hand only received a small, red mark underneath my thumb. It is my belief that the necklace had been balanced on top of the curtains or the curtain pole, although I will never know for sure. This incident was certainly unexpected and a little disquieting. I know Elizabeth would never intend to hurt me, the necklace just happened to fall onto my hand.

On another occasion, I was getting ready for work and part of my daily routine included using a foot spray to keep my feet cool and fresh. I collected it from the bathroom and then made my way to the bedroom. When I pulled the lid off the foot spray, my necklace came plummeting out and proceeded to land on my foot. It made me jump and I shouted a profanity that I won't repeat. What's more, I was amazed at what had taken place. Absolutely gobsmacked. At least my necklace had been returned so I could wear it once again.

Another time, two petits pains were cooking in the oven for Mia's breakfast. As they looked lightly browned, I decided it was time to take them out. I reached for an oven glove and naturally took the top one of the two. Slipping my hand inside, I felt something at the end of my fingertips. I was so surprised when this happened that I quickly removed my hand. Inside the glove, was my necklace. I was at a loss for words. Elizabeth must have known that I would use the oven glove that day, although it was such an unusual place to put it. The necklace had been in my bedroom drawer the evening before but had gone missing by the time I had woken up.

It came as no surprise, when I reached for my necklace in the bedroom drawer and found it wasn't there. Gone. It had gone again. I wondered where it would be this time. My day went on as usual and evening came. In the living room, Graham and Mia decided to have a cushion fight. (Well, it was the next best thing to a pillow fight.) He picked up a plump, white cushion and was about to throw it at Mia when he stopped dead in his tracks. There was something hard inside the cover.

Unzipping it, he found my necklace neatly tucked away in one of the corners. Elizabeth must have intended Graham to find it instead of me for a change.

I was about to go out and went to put the keys away. My handbag at the time had many different compartments. It was in one of these compartments that I discovered my necklace. I felt astonished, especially because it was still zipped up. How had Elizabeth known I would put my keys in the very same place as the necklace? Only minutes before, it had been on the black coffee table in the living room. I had popped upstairs to use the bathroom and after coming back down I had intended to put my necklace on. In that short space of time, Elizabeth had moved it.

Other bits and bobs were in the bedroom drawer but not my necklace. I glanced around the room to see if it was there. It was nowhere in sight. Perhaps the necklace was somewhere else in the house, waiting for me to find it. Then a thought crossed my mind, I wondered if Elizabeth had taken possession of the necklace and hadn't yet decided where to put it. I understand it takes a great deal of energy for a spirit to move an object because they can't pick it up like you and I can. Some spirits can't move objects at all. What is clear is that Elizabeth's energy is strong and sometimes she demonstrated this by moving larger objects, which I will tell you about later in the book. I had this feeling though, that the necklace was in the bedroom somewhere. For that reason, I decided to have a more thorough look around and it was then that I saw it.

My bedroom walls were painted sunshine yellow with that awful masonry paint with the sand in it. It was the previous owner's choice, certainly not my cup of tea. I find it can scratch your skin with ease if you brush yourself against its protruding clusters of sharp sand. My necklace was dangling from one of the aforementioned clusters of sand. I couldn't believe what I was seeing. Taking it down, I couldn't work out how the necklace had remained on the sand. Out of curiosity, I tried to place it back in the same position but it wouldn't stay there. When I attempted this again, it fell to the carpet below. This happened every single time so I knew it was impossible for the necklace to hang from there. How on earth had Elizabeth done it? When I tried to put it back in the same spot, it was impossible for it to stay there. Each time, it fell to the floor. I was bewildered, unable to find an answer. On numerous occasions, I had been unable to replicate the situation. I really don't know how Elizabeth can do this but I can't. Then again, maybe this is something we are never meant to know. As I see it, spirit is far more advanced than us.

I mentioned earlier on that I had bought my necklace from Boscastle, Cornwall. It was on this very same occasion that I also acquired an unusual and eye-catching mantle clock. Standing at twenty-eight centimetres high, it is pewter, surrealist, and Dali inspired. Even though it was meant for the mantelpiece, I didn't have one. Instead, the clock was placed on top of a bookcase where it always kept good time. It was just as well really because I haven't got a wall clock or any other clock in the living room for that matter. Fortunately, it didn't look out of place with the furnishings, standing proud, as if it belonged there.

Eventually, I felt awake enough to pull back the duvet and take myself away from my cosy bed. I got dressed. Then I rummaged through the bedroom drawer and noticed my necklace was missing. Not thinking anymore of it, I hurried downstairs to get some breakfast. It was on the way to the kitchen that I glanced at the clock and it was then that I caught sight of it. I was stunned. With its gleaming chain wrapped around the minute hand, was my necklace. Vibrant red rubies sparkled as the sun shone through the window. Weighed down, the imprisoned hand had ceased moving. Perhaps Elizabeth was reminding me to take some time out and relax, as I do tend to rush here, there and everywhere trying to get as much done as possible.

She has no facial features but looks beautiful. Her head is bowed, with hands in the prayer position and wings wrapped around her lower body. I purchased this angel ornament from a gift shop in the village of Burley in the New Forest, Hampshire. It was some years back now.

The previous evening, I had put my necklace away as usual in the bedroom drawer. By the time morning came, it was gone. I knew it would make an appearance, what I didn't know was where or when. Morning continued and nothing out of the ordinary presented itself to me. Finding my necklace was one of the last things on my mind as I carried on with the day's routine. Afternoon came. As I often did, I dusted the little mahogany table in the living room and it was then that I noticed my necklace. What surprised me was that the loosely wound chain was around the angel ornaments neck, whilst the cross-hung neatly in her robed lap. The first thought that crossed my mind was the word significance. Was it meaningful, important to me?

After a period of reflection, I had no doubt it was important to me as I had found my cherished necklace but what did the placing of it actually mean? Was an angel looking out for me or did Elizabeth have a fondness for angels or that particular ornament? I cannot answer these questions because I never did get around to asking her. Maybe I should have. Maybe I still should. More importantly though, it made me feel privileged and blessed that a spirit would use so much energy to move my necklace and present this to me.

Often, I thought about getting a bedside lamp but I never did get around to buying one, although I wish I had. On one occasion, I clearly remember fumbling around in the dark to put my necklace away in my bedroom drawer. I heard it drop down safely and knew it was where it should be. Shortly afterwards, I settled down to go to sleep. It wasn't until the following evening that I discovered my necklace dangling from the ceiling lampshade. I had flicked the switch to turn the light on and there it was, resting next to the light bulb. Had Elizabeth read my thoughts? It seemed strange that she had put the necklace in that place and at that particular time.

Another location that Elizabeth liked to move my necklace to, was the banister post at the top of the first flight of stairs. It would always be lying flat upon the post and not once was it suspended from or wrapped around the post. She never put it on any of the other ones either. Luckily, I always noticed the necklace before putting my hand on the post, which I usually do when walking up and down the stairs. Otherwise, it might have startled me.

It was morning. After sitting down to watch television, I came across it. My necklace had unexpectedly turned up on the arm of the old, blue settee. Positioned ruby side up, the polished chain was neatly laid out. It was so beautifully arranged. Was Elizabeth trying to tell me something? I couldn't see a connection with anything though.

On another morning, I'd made my way downstairs when I set eyes upon my necklace. Beforehand, I had gone to put it on but it was missing from the bedroom drawer. On entering the living room, I happened to look up to the right and it was then that my necklace came into view. Imagine my surprise. It was hanging down from a picture hook behind one of the canvas prints. As a matter of fact, it was the first place my gaze had been directed to.

Usually, you would expect to find an empty glass or one filled with liquid of some description. Well, this pint glass stood in the kitchen cupboard with something a little bit different in it. My necklace, crumpled in a heap, looked completely alien. What could Elizabeth mean by this? Did I drink too little, too much or none of these. Was it a message? I really didn't know.

A fluffy, red teddy bear; it sat on my bedside unit, smiling as always. Why wouldn't it? Life was good for him because he had nothing to worry about. Waking up after a peaceful night's sleep, I didn't even need to look in the bedroom drawer. My necklace was clearly visible as it shone in the sunlight, streaming in above the velvet curtains. Some of the plastic hooks had come loose, leaving a baggy opening which had rudely awoken me. Please don't get me wrong, I love sunshine but not at that unearthly hour of the morning. The curtains needed fixing.

Highlighting the bear, I could clearly make out he was wearing a necklace. Not any old necklace but mine. The chain was wrapped twice around its neck and the visible cross dangled down a little. Red rubies upon red; it was camouflaged to a degree but I had still noticed it. Not a lot escapes me.

Two acoustic guitars on stands are displayed in the living room. The lights were low and from a distance, I recognised the outline of my necklace. It was suspended, supported by the tuning key above. Graham and Mia play guitar more often than myself so it seemed odd that I was the one to find it. Did Elizabeth want me to play? Then again, she could have been having fun and put it there for the purpose of amusement.

I was nearing the end of this chapter, which is mainly about phenomenon associated with my necklace, when it disappeared again. With its chain twisted, I discovered it inside the glass-fronted cabinet in the living room. Was Elizabeth sending me a sign? Perhaps she was showing her support for my writing.

Chapter 5
Magnetic Forces

Something that fascinates me is the paranormal interaction I've experienced with fridge magnets. A refrigerator magnet or fridge magnet as is more commonly known, is an ornament attached to a small magnet. It is used to post items such as children's pictures, photographs, shopping lists and the like on a refrigerator door. However, many people collect fridge magnets and solely use them for decorative display. Also, they are favoured souvenir objects and come in many shapes and sizes.

Plastic letter fridge magnets have been manufactured since the 1960s and marketed as an educational invention for young children. These come in a set and are usually bright and colourful, therefore appealing to youngsters. They are ideal for early letter recognition and the spelling of simple words or phrases. Many years ago, I bought one of these sets for Mia and Sam to help them with their learning. It was purchased from a well-known toy retailer.

Strangely, it wasn't long afterwards, that Elizabeth first started to form words with the letters. In the beginning, I dismissed it as being her and placed the blame upon the children. This appeared the obvious choice at the time because the letters had spelt out 'mum and dad'. When they denied doing this, it was Graham who got the brunt of it, because he was the only one left in the household who could have done it. Was he joking around? When I asked him if he was, he categorically replied, "No." I knew he was telling me the truth. Call it instinct, but I could always tell.

It appeared that Elizabeth was trying to communicate with me through using the fridge magnets. However, I wasn't her mum but perhaps I reminded her of her mum. Maybe that's why she felt drawn towards me. Likewise, Graham may have resembled her dad in many ways.

Some weeks later, I became aware of two more messages. 'Take care of Dad' and 'Dad is sad', one placed underneath the other. Funnily enough, this made complete sense at the time because Graham had been feeling particularly down in the dumps. Subsequently, Elizabeth spelt out 'Mum is bad' and I thoroughly understood why. Don't get me wrong, I'm not a horrible person but at the time it was relevant to the situation. I have always valued Elizabeth's opinion and insight, as spirits seem to understand exactly what is taking place in a person's life.

It was two days after Christmas in 2013, when another message was bestowed upon me. At some point during the morning, the vivid colours of the fridge magnets had caught my attention. My astonished eyes rested on the words 'Be happy'. Although it was in amongst the swirl of magnets that surrounded it, the message stood out loud and clear. One of the most remarkable facts about it was that I could relate to it.

That same cold day, we were due to visit Graham's mum. When the time came, we settled in our car ready for the journey and I turned the radio on. The station was playing a song called 'Happy' by Pharrell Williams, which I had never heard before. Despite this, it hit the number one spot in the charts later that week. Surprisingly, I heard the word 'happy' almost immediately upon listening. It is said that spirits can communicate with us by synchronicities and one way of doing this is through music. I'm sure this was validation for the message I had received earlier. I was truly amazed.

On another occasion, I was in the kitchen doing some chores before going to work. As my mind wandered from one thought to another, my gaze steadily fell upon the left-hand side of the fridge. The many-coloured magnets spelt out two simple words 'Cheer up'. Leading up to this event, I had been feeling rather low in mood and negative about life in general. Some people cannot abide being told to 'Cheer up' by others. In my view, I saw it as a positive sign that Elizabeth wanted to help and support me. Grateful for her concern, I smiled to myself. To be honest, she never failed to astonish me. Elizabeth knew exactly how I felt and I could hide nothing from her, for she always knew.

Fiery. What does that word mean to you? It depends on the context, doesn't it? The words presented to me read 'Beware of the man with the fiery hair'. This colourful array of fridge magnets conveyed something that made me think very carefully. Hair having the bright colour of fire. I envisioned the flames. My initial thoughts of red turned to orange and then it clicked. Ginger. That was it, Ginger. All of a sudden, I realised exactly who Elizabeth was talking about.

He was a man I knew at work, although I cannot name him for confidentiality reasons. At the time, I had started work as a teaching assistant at a local school and he was a teacher. When I received the message, I was puzzled as to why I should beware of him. There was certainly nothing I felt worried about. Confused, I knew it meant something important, but what? It was a warning. A warning I had to try and figure out.

Time passed. I knew that the best thing to do was to try and communicate with Elizabeth to find out the meaning of the message. Feeling hopeful, I called out a number of times on different occasions but unfortunately didn't receive a response. What I do know is that a spirit is not like a performing seal and cannot always come through with the click of a finger. It requires energy and sometimes that energy just isn't there whenever we wish to speak to them.

The night of the school disco had arrived and it was almost time for Mia to be collected from her class. I asked Graham if he could fetch her, as I was busy doing jobs around the house. On her return, Mia told me all about her exciting evening. Even though I had still been trying to make contact with Elizabeth, it had been to no avail.

The next day, I called out to her once again. She knocked. I felt over the moon that she was with me. Desperate to find out the meaning of the message, I asked numerous questions until I was able to piece the answers together. It transpired that had I gone and collected Mia from the disco, I would have been personally handed a mobile number written on a piece of paper. His mobile number. The man with the fiery hair. As it was, Graham had picked Mia up, although it should have been me. Strangely, the only reason I didn't go was that Graham was available and I had something that I really needed to get done. Although it may not seem like much to beware of, who knows what might have happened if I had been given that telephone number and what events may have unfolded.

It was in 1973 that the mobile phone was invented, many years after the end of the Victorian era. Nowadays, it is an invention that most people cannot live without. My next message would refer to this device as a 'Wrong box' and I can understand exactly where Elizabeth was coming from with this name. After having nearly being given the teachers mobile number, I believe she thought of it as a negative object.

As I see it, the invention of the mobile phone is marvellous in some respects but not so great in others. I know that as well as being the bearer of positive news, it could also bring about unfavourable news. Some people use them as a tool that can cause heartache and arguments if the temptation is there. Before long, social media evolved and would only reinforce this notion. The term 'Wrong box' was such a simple term, yet it captured the essence of Elizabeth's thoughts completely.

I looked steadily and intently at the centre of the fridge door as the words 'Journey's end' stared back at me in an assortment of rainbow colours. My mind immediately wondered. Searching on the Internet, I was eager to find out what this message could possibly mean. It didn't take long for me to realise. A stopping place or destination; the place one wants to go. I felt it signified the following of a particular path in life, given that we all have free will in what we choose to do.

At the time, an ex-boyfriend of seven years had contacted me and was keen for me to meet up with him. Sadly, he had decided to end our relationship fifteen years before, so to say I was shocked at hearing from him was an understatement. I declined his offer. Thinking back, I believe that we spend a lifetime searching for true love and it is in finding our love that we don't have to look anymore. It is then that particular journey will end. Elizabeth was communicating with me that my journey's end was with Graham and that I had made the right decision.

Arriving back home after a morning of Christmas shopping with Graham, I made my way to the kitchen. It was there and then that I noticed it. A message. Although it was not a message that I understood. The words 'Too much gatter' were surrounded by all the other many-hued fridge magnets. Gatter was not a word that I recognised, in fact I had never encountered it before. I thought really hard but still could not make heads of tails of it. Perhaps Elizabeth was mistaken and had meant to choose a similar word. Did she mean chatter? I'm a talkative person so should it of read 'Too much chatter?' However, I wasn't convinced.

I went through the whole alphabet trying to think of words that it could be. None of them made any real sense in context of the sentence. It was then that I wondered if the letters 'c' and 'h' were missing from the fridge. If they were, she could have used the 'g' instead to spell the word chatter. Carefully, I looked but both the letters were there. This could only mean one thing, the word 'gatter' must be spelt correctly. Elizabeth's spellings were always spot on.

A thought came into my mind like a bolt from the blue. Could it be a Victorian word? Straightaway, I decided to do some research on the Internet and typed in the words Victorian language. On doing this, the term Victorian slang stared back at me from the screen. Swiftly, I scrolled down the pages until I came to the letter G. Feeling excited, my eyes fell upon the word 'gatter'. It was there in black and white. At last, I had found the answer. Beer, it was slang for beer. My initial thought was that Elizabeth was a cheeky so and so for implying I was having too much of my favourite drink. I was the adult after all and she was the child! Mind you, spirits are so much more enlightened than us, that it was for this reason that I knew to always listen to her advice. Christmas Day was one week away and I had a two-week holiday from work, so I had been indulging a little more than I normally would. I'm not sure if Elizabeth was telling me off or warning me against over drinking but either way, I knew it was an important message for me to adhere to.

It was my lunch break at work and as usual I returned home to let my two dogs out in the garden. On entering the kitchen, I was astonished to see fridge magnets laid out on top of the work surfaces. This in itself was unusual as previous messages had always been placed on the fridge door. Strangely, they were positioned either side of the oven. They certainly hadn't been there when I'd left the house that morning. I looked closely. The message read, 'Spirit Box ten o'clock'. Fortunately, this made complete sense to me as I have a spirit box which I could use at that time of evening. I will explain what a spirit box is for those of you that haven't heard of it before.

There have been various technologies used to record the voices or sounds of spirits, the spirit box being one of them. This device was invented in 2002 by a man named Frank Sumption and was known as a Frank's box. Nowadays, it is often referred to as a spirit box or ghost box and is used as an electronic medium to directly communicate with a spirit. It is a modified portable AM/FM radio that quickly and continually scans the radio stations. As the channels are swept through, a mix of white noise and audio fragments can be audibly heard. These fragments consist of music, human speech or whatever is being broadcast at the time the radio sweep is made. The spirit then uses this material to create its own voices.

Not everything that comes through is spirit box communication, some of it will be radio noise. It can take a lot of time and practice to know the difference and to be able to hear the messages. I always record the sessions and listen to them afterwards, as it is clearer to hear them this way as opposed to real time. The idea of using white noise to allow spirits to speak is nothing new. I have been using a spirit box for many years now and I am well acquainted with how they work.

Let us return to the message that said 'Spirit Box ten o'clock'. It appeared that Elizabeth wanted to communicate with me through this device and I was more than willing to try this at the time she had requested. Feeling positive that I would get exceptional results, I left home to go back to work. I was confident about what was to come.

Later that evening, I promptly set up the spirit box ready for the highly anticipated ten o'clock session. I lit a candle, as I always do and waited. When the time came, I spoke some words of protection to open the session. Respectfully, I asked for positive spirits from the white light to come forward and for them to protect me from any negative spirits. Then I called out clearly, "Elizabeth, are you here?" I gave her some time to acknowledge the question, as spirit cannot always reply immediately. There was no answer. I then repeated the question but all I could hear was the radio noise. Still, I continued to ask further questions, none of which had a response. Feeling despondent, I assumed she wasn't with me.

To say I was confused, was an understatement. Why would Elizabeth send me a message saying that she wanted to speak to me at ten o'clock, if she wasn't going to be there? Perhaps something urgent had occurred in the spirit realm that she had to attend to, or could it be that she didn't have enough energy to use the spirit box. There had to be a valid reason why, I just didn't know what it was. After twenty minutes, it was time to close the session down. I thanked Elizabeth for trying to come through and turned the spirit box off. There would be other opportunities for us to communicate.

It is to my knowledge that there is no concept of time in the spirit world. Ten years to us could pass as quick as a flash to a spirit. This proved true one day when I caught sight of a message sprawled in colourful magnets across the fridge door. Surprisingly, it said 'Cornwall soon'. I certainly hadn't made any plans to travel there at that particular time or in the near future.

Soon afterwards, this concept drifted to the back of my mind. It wasn't until a few years later at Christmas, that my parents kindly gave Graham and me a sum of money to spend on a holiday of our choice. We chose Cornwall. That summer we had a fabulous two-week stay in a beautiful cottage. Even though this was connected to 'Cornwall', my gut instinct told me this wasn't what Elizabeth meant by that message. I have always wanted to move to Cornwall and settle down but this is something I cannot afford. Therefore, I still hope that Elizabeth can foresee that I will live there one day.

As I was sitting in the kitchen starting to write this chapter, a spinner landed next to me on the laminate floor. I recognised the familiar noise and knew straightaway what it was. When I looked in the glass-fronted cabinet in the living room, I noticed that the other spinner was missing from its place. It was a little later on in the evening when I spotted it on top of my notepad, which was situated on the dinner table. Maybe it was Elizabeth encouraging me to continue writing.

Chapter 6
Strange Goings-On

I can, without doubt, tell the difference between a human sneeze and a sneeze made by a dog, which leads me onto my next encounter with the paranormal. It was raining hard in the evening and the old-fashioned, gas fire was on in the living room. I needed to dry and warm myself after having just walked the dogs. As I sat near the warmth of the flickering flames, I quickly rubbed my cold hands together. The obliging heat was much appreciated.

Baya was resting in the kitchen and Freddie was outside in the garden, when I heard a sneeze nearby in the living room. Immediately, I thought it sounded like the kind of sneeze Baya would make but then I remembered she wasn't in the room. Graham heard it at the same time and also thought it was Baya sneezing. I'm convinced it was the spirit of Boy as he had visited us many times before, especially during the winter months when we had the heating on. We were amazed by what we had listened to.

My side of the bed has been the focus of a great deal of paranormal activity. I have found popcorn kernels underneath the duvet, on top of the duvet, underneath the pillow and on top of the pillow. Strangely, the same can be said for the spinners, as I would find them in identical places. Most often, this would occur as I was about to get into bed for the night.

One April afternoon, I went upstairs to my bedroom and was taken aback by what I saw. All of the objects on the drawer unit next to the bed (my side) had been rearranged. It was a wondrous sight and I was astonished. Everything was lined up neat and orderly. There were two photographs, one of my brother and I when we were younger and another of Mia with my nan. They had been placed next to each other on top of my pink pencil case. What was remarkable was the fact that the photo of my brother and me had previously fallen down the back of the drawer unit and now it was propped up high on display. Nine ornaments had been moved around, as had a box of paper clips, some perfume, an alarm clock, an iPod charger, a telephone, two piggy banks and two teddy bears. It must have taken a great deal of energy for Elizabeth to have moved all of these items.

After arriving home, Mia entered the living room and as she did, she noticed that a canvas picture had been turned upside down. It was the image of a single, red rose and the stem was facing downwards. This came as no surprise to me, as I knew that Elizabeth was capable of moving many different objects. Mia though, was taken aback.

Lunchtime came. I'd popped home from work and it was then that I discovered a canvas picture of five, red tulips had been rotated upside down. As before, this had occurred in the living room. Being in a rush, I left it as it was. When I returned home later that afternoon, it was back to normal as it had been placed the right way up. It stopped me in my tracks.

On another occasion, I went downstairs and had just set foot in the living room, when I felt an overwhelming desire to look straight ahead of me. There and then, I became aware that a canvas picture of an angel was upside down. It was one Mia had painted for me some time before and it held a special place in my heart. My other angel canvas picture, which was painted by Sam, remained untouched.

Returning home from the supermarket, I hastily deposited a twenty-pound note on one of the arms of the settee. I'd intended to put it in my purse after I'd unpacked all the food shopping. At one stage, I went upstairs and when I came back down, I noticed something resting on top of the picture hook that was next to the door leading to the stairs. Feeling curious, I edged nearer. On closer inspection, I saw it was a twenty-pound note. A crisp twenty-pound note. It transpired it was the very same one that I had left on the arm of the settee since it was no longer there.

Up my stairs and along the landing, I have various wooden framed pictures. As it happened, two of these ended up exchanging places but they weren't moved by human hands. One of these pictures was a field full of beautiful poppies and the other was an embroidery of a ship that Graham had made when he was little. It was late one afternoon, when I first noticed they had changed position.

Spectacularly, this was the first time that pictures had actually been removed and switched around. By the evening, Elizabeth had moved them back to their original location. Subsequently, I was left speechless as you can imagine.

As I pulled the covers were pulled back, it revealed the blackness of two Japanese scroll paintings. Beforehand, they had been hanging on the landing wall. Now they were carefully placed on my side of the bed. What on earth! It amazed me once again, that Elizabeth had the spiritual energy to move these items and I wondered if there was a meaning behind this. Was she trying to tell me something?

It was first thing in the morning and I came downstairs. Opening the living room door, I became aware that the guitar I kept nearest to the porch door was now placed in front of it. Facing me, it stood on its black stand. I knew it was Elizabeth because the children had gone to bed before us and were still fast asleep. Feeling astonished, I carefully placed it where it belonged. It had moved approximately one metre.

A few days later, while watching television with Graham, I heard what I can only describe as a 'dong' sound. Deep and resonate, it appeared to be coming from the direction of my late granddad's guitar. Amazingly, it sounded like the lowest note was being plucked several times. Initially, Graham had thought it was a broken string that had made the noise but when it happened more than once, he realised that wasn't the case.

Late one afternoon, Graham and I were in the living room attempting to entertain Baya and Freddie. We had already taken them for a long walk but they were still bored, and needed to work off some excess energy. For some reason, there wasn't a dog toy in sight for them to play with. After a thorough search of the room, we assumed they were either hidden somewhere else or in the back garden.

As I was about to head off to have a look, a yellow ball slowly rolled out from under the two-seater settee. It stopped in front of my feet. Only a moment before, I had mentioned that the dogs didn't have a ball and could do with one. Surprisingly, my request had been answered. Elizabeth had been listening. I had carefully checked underneath both the leather settees and there hadn't been a single thing there. The ball was one that belonged to the dogs but it had appeared out of nowhere. As you can imagine, Baya and Freddie were overjoyed and immediately began to play with it.

Another occurrence took place in the kitchen while I was writing this book. Graham was preparing some food and I was busy typing. Suddenly, we both heard a loud noise. I thought it came from either behind the rubbish bin or under the sink unit which are positioned next to each other. Wondering what had caused the noise, I looked behind the bin but there was nothing there. Meanwhile, Graham rummaged about under the sink. It was there he found it. A small power ball. I had seen it in a drawer of the glass-fronted cabinet only the day before. It must have been thrown with force across the kitchen and then rolled underneath. The power ball hadn't come into contact with us and I know Elizabeth would never cause us any harm. She obviously wanted to let us know she was there. Subsequently, I acknowledged Elizabeth and thanked her for the sign.

I have various bouncy balls in the house which Mia and Sam used to play with when they were younger. Nowadays, they are stored away in the living room. There is one particular ball which would constantly turn up in places I would find it.

Places like the washing basket, nestled in between the freshly cleaned linen. Now, I wouldn't mind if it was a plain coloured bouncy ball but this one has a witches face on it which frightens the life out of me.

I'm sure Elizabeth doesn't mean to scare me. I believe she thought it was amusing to see my reaction each time. It was as if Elizabeth was playing a joke on me. She is a spirit child after all.

Like many people, I have created an angel altar. I keep my collection of angels on the middle shelf in my glass-fronted cabinet. It consists of an angel trinket box, [which I talked about earlier in the book] two large statues, two small statues, three pendants, two necklaces, two letter openers and last but not least a little, paper photograph of my late granddad. I love this calm and welcoming space.

As it was a workday, I returned home as usual for my lunch break. At one point, I casually glanced over at my beloved angels and it was then that I noticed the two large statues were laid face down on the shelf. On closer inspection, I could see that the two smaller statues were facing back to front. In addition, the photograph of my late granddad had been moved to the shelf above. Feeling apprehensive, I left the house to return to work.

When I arrived home later that afternoon, my initial thought was to look at the statues. I was stunned to find them back to normal, standing straight and facing in the right direction. However, my treasured photograph was still on the shelf above so I placed it back with the angels and my arrangement was complete. What could the significance of this be? It was difficult to understand why this had happened. I wondered if I had done something or someone wrong because the angels had turned their backs on me.

Teddy bears. Most children love them and I'm sure spirit children find them endearing too, as Elizabeth does. As I see it, she has always enjoyed playing games with them. I found it interesting where Elizabeth would hide them.

It was morning and time for me to go to work. Picking up my brown handbag, I noticed something odd. At first I thought I could see what looked like a considerable sized ball of red fluff. Close up, I could see this was not the case. One of Mia's teddy bears stared back at me. It was so funny, I started to laugh. All I could think of was that he was hitching a ride. Half of its shaggy arm was limply hanging out of one of the compartments. The teddy usually sits on top of my bedroom drawer unit and I had seen it there the night before.

Before long, I had another experience involving a teddy bear and it came about because I asked Elizabeth to give me a sign. I suggested that she could send me a message using the fridge magnets but it seemed Elizabeth had another idea. Soon afterwards I left for work. The morning passed.

When I arrived home at lunchtime, I opened the creaky living room door and a grey teddy came tumbling down from above. It landed clumsily on the wooden floor a little way ahead of me. My first thought was that Graham had played a trick on me and had left the teddy balanced on top of the door. Then I looked closely and realised there was no possible way it could've stayed there without falling off. Furthermore, I remembered that the door had been shut tight so there was no room to position the teddy. Elizabeth. It had to be Elizabeth. This was the sign that I'd asked for. One of the interesting things about it was the message on the t-shirt of the teddy. The words read 'I want you to know just how much I love you'. I felt so blessed and smiled to myself before thanking Elizabeth for her kind token.

On another occasion, I opened the living room door and found the green and white cushions stacked up high. I had been the last person to go to bed the previous evening and as part of my usual routine I'd plumped and straightened all the cushions, making sure they were in the correct place. Now they stood as tall as a tree on the seat of the three-seater settee. I was really taken aback by what I saw. They were beautifully poised. It must have taken an immense amount of energy for Elizabeth to have moved them.

On my return from the bathroom, I casually opened the living room door and a black pen fell from above. At full tilt, it brushed lightly against my arm on its journey downward. Straight away, I picked the pen up. It felt warm to the touch. As I went to sit down, I realised the pen I'd been writing with was missing from its place. I had left it on top of my writing pad, which I had been using before I went upstairs. It came as no surprise that it looked exactly like the one that had fallen to the ground.

As it happens, I do like to scribble and I often sit down with my pen and writing pad nearby. One evening, while at the dining room table, I had been jotting down various notes and I decided to take a bit of a break. Five minutes passed and I returned to continue my writing, when I discovered that the black pen I had been using was standing upright. Oddly, a white, plastic clothes peg was clasped around the middle section of the pen. This was very unexpected. I'm not sure why Elizabeth did this but it certainly grabbed my attention. No matter how hard I tried, I could not make the pen stand up again.

At one time, I used to own giant African land snails. I was replacing the snail's vegetarian food, when I heard a strange, continuous noise on the wooden floor. Feeling puzzled, I peered under the dining room table but there was nothing in sight. As the sound persisted, I listened carefully to see where it was coming from. In next to no time, I moved towards the double radiator and it was then that I saw a large, dark coloured marble rolling towards me. There was no one around, as the children were out and Graham was in our bedroom recording a video. I recognised the glossy marble. It was one that I kept on the living room bookshelf but it couldn't have fallen, as it usually sat in a deep groove in the wood.

One afternoon, Graham and I were in the kitchen getting ready to go food shopping, while Mia and her friend, Alice, were sitting in the living room. Suddenly, an empty, plastic drinks bottle fell off the work surface which was next to the pedal bin. It made quite a noise but then I also heard the bin opening and closing. This made me jump, and I was surprised to say the least. Immediately, Graham looked and found the bin lid was down. Inside, lay the bottle. Elizabeth must have had some fun with this escapade. If only all of my rubbish could clear itself away like that!

My necklace with the cross, isn't the only piece of jewellery that Elizabeth has been associated with. It is fortunate that I wear three rings which are very special to me, my engagement ring, wedding ring and eternity ring. Therefore, I only remove them if I really have to and on such occasions some strange things occurred. I seldom suffer from water retention, which causes my fingers to swell but when I do, I have to take my rings off. It was on one such occasion that I had removed them and left them on top of the unit in the living room.

A couple of days passed, and I noticed that the swelling had subsided so I went to put the rings back on. Although two of the rings were there, my wedding ring was missing. My first port of call was with my family, to see if anyone had moved it. They hadn't. Then I hunted high and low in and around the area that I'd left the ring but still to no avail. I was getting more and more worried by the minute, so I thoroughly checked both the settees, in case the ring had accidently got knocked down the side of the arm or in between the seats. It wasn't there. Hesitant to do so, I decided to stop the search only to resume it at a later time. Slowly, I took a deep breath, hoping that Elizabeth would be able to help find the ring and return it to me. I called out loud.

About an hour later, I continued looking. For some strange reason, I felt compelled to look at the unit. It's as if I was being guided in that direction. I glanced over with the opinion that I could see all three rings on the side, although part of me still doubted myself. As I gradually moved closer, the gleaming wedding ring came into view. It was back in its original place along with the two other rings. I felt ecstatic. Standing there, I thanked Elizabeth over and over again for her help in returning the ring.

Unfortunately, it wasn't long before I suffered with water retention again so I placed my three rings on the middle shelf of the glass-fronted cabinet for safekeeping. Every now and then I checked to make sure they were still there. The next day arrived and I looked again. It came as no surprise to find that both my wedding ring and eternity ring were missing. My family hadn't touched them so I knew it was Elizabeth that had borrowed them. I say 'borrowed' because they would be returned to me.

Feeling bewildered as to why Elizabeth would want the rings, I left the wedding ring where it was. By nightfall, that too had disappeared. When I awoke the following morning, the first thing I did was to go downstairs to see if the rings had reappeared. There sat the eternity ring, all by itself. The swelling in my fingers had disappeared so I placed the ring back on. A few days later, both the other rings came back, returned to the exact same place I had left them.

As I see it, Elizabeth has taken a particular liking to my jewellery, as well as all the other objects I've talked about in this book. I'm aware that she is a strong, positive energy who surrounds me with love. She has this vibrancy about her and she loves to play games. Games that would continue.

Chapter 7
More Strange Goings-On

Justice. This is a card in the Major Arcana in a deck of tarot cards. For those of you that don't know, the Major Arcana deals with the human condition. Each card represents the ups and downs that every person will experience during their lifetime. I often do readings for family members, although I'm not an expert and use a book to guide me.

Unexpectedly, this card turned up on top of my mobile phone, picture side up. Elizabeth later confirmed she had placed it there. It depicts a female figure holding scales and a sword. My illustration shows this but she is a sad looking woman, in a long, white robe sitting on a golden throne. A wise owl is perched on her left shoulder. There are two, sturdy pillars either side of her.

Justice can appear in answer to questions associated with the law, contracts or formal agreements. It can also symbolise signatures required on legal documents, negotiations or a court case. This card, (if face up like mine was,) suggests that a legal dispute would be resolved in my favour. I thought long and hard but there was nothing I could relate it to at that time. Strangely enough, it wasn't until some months later that it all made sense as tarot can predict the future as well as the present.

I have signed a disclaimer to say that I will never discuss my legal case but what I can tell you is that it did involve a contract, an arbiter and it almost went to court. Luckily, the outcome was favourable, with me accepting compensation. All of these areas were predicted by the Justice card that Elizabeth gave me. Spirits can see what is ahead of us and although they cannot change free will, she was aware of what I would have to go through.

As we know, Elizabeth likes to hide things and our Satnav (satellite navigation) was one of them. At the time, we had a portable Satnav, instead of one that was built into our car. We were due to go on a journey and it would tell us where we were and how to get to our destination. Graham had left the Satnav on the side of the television stand and was about to program the address in it when he realised it had gone. He asked me if I had moved it and of course I said no, as did the children. Adamant he had left the Satnav there, he was completely baffled.

Thinking it must have fallen down the back of the stand, Graham took a few steps forward and directed his gaze around the corner. There was just a mass of black cables. He couldn't understand where it could be. I on the other hand, had my suspicions.

As the evening progressed, Graham became increasingly worried because the Satnav was needed for the following morning. Unhappily, I told him that I would have to resort to the archaic method of reading a map. It wasn't the end of the world but I asked Elizabeth out loud that if she did have it, could she please return it to us, as we needed it as soon as possible. We waited.

It was late and the time came for us to go to bed. We had intended to go earlier so we would feel refreshed for our trip. Instead, we had been waiting, hoping the Satnav would turn up. It hadn't. Feeling despondent, I pointed the remote control at the television to turn it off. Suddenly, something caught my eye. Resting on top of the stand was the Satnav, as though it hadn't been anywhere. Relieved, I thanked Elizabeth, especially because we wouldn't have to fret about it overnight.

Another device that went missing was my mobile phone. I often leave it in the same spot and this occasion didn't differ from the norm. It sat alongside a slim line lamp, on top of a little mahogany table. One overcast evening, I went to get my mobile. Reaching out to pick it up, I discovered it wasn't in its place. I asked Mia and Sam if they had seen it and as I expected, they both said no. Graham had gone out so I knew he wasn't involved in any way.

Confused, I was one hundred per cent sure that I had not misplaced my mobile. Although I knew it was pointless, I scoured the living room but it was nowhere to be found. Therefore, one thought came to mind. Elizabeth. It must be Elizabeth that had whisked the mobile away. I hoped it wouldn't be gone for too long.

Graham returned home so I explained to him what had happened. Helpfully, he suggested that he could try phoning my mobile to see if it was in the house. I went upstairs, while Graham stayed downstairs. Then he rang the number. Intently, we listened. Silence. There was nothing to be heard.

The evening passed and the mobile was still missing. I needed to get some sleep, so I decided to head up to bed. Looking forward to settling down on the comfortable mattress, I pulled back the freshly washed bedcovers. Then I became aware of it. Neatly placed in the middle of my pillow as if in wait for me, was my mobile. Its blue light flashed repeatedly. Words cannot describe how I felt. I presumed that the flashing light was down to the fact that Graham had tried to phone it. Feeling curious, I picked my mobile up and entered my passcode. It revealed a missed call. Graham's missed call. Despite the fact the ringtone was on full volume, it hadn't rung out loud while I'd been upstairs. This led me to believe that at some point, Elizabeth had taken it with her to the spirit realm. I was grateful that my mobile had been returned to me sooner rather than later.

It was the morning of the residential trip, and Sam was due to go to Fairthorne Manor with his school. The previous day, I had taken great care in packing most of his personal belongings, neatly ticking the items off my list as I went along.

Meticulously, I made sure the last of his things had been placed into his trolley suitcase, his blue toothbrush being one of them. There were always some bits and bobs you couldn't pack the night before! Then I zipped up the case, it was full to capacity.

We awaited the arrival of Sam's then best friend, Connor, who was also going on the trip with him. Meanwhile, Graham left for work and Mia went off to school with her friend. In next to no time, the doorbell rang. It was Connor, accompanied by his oversized rucksack. Excitedly, he came in and sat down. Then we made conversation about the activities that Fairthorne Manor had to offer.

The time came for me to take Sam and Connor over to the school. After making sure they had everything that was needed, I reached for my keys. They weren't there. I had left them on the arm of the three-seater settee, having only checked a few minutes earlier. Bewildered, I questioned the boys and asked if they had seen them. Both replied, "No."

As a matter of urgency, I felt down the inner side of the arm and underneath the settee cushion. My fingertips could feel nothing except for the softness of the fabric. Looking behind the settee and on the surrounding floor area, I still couldn't find the keys. Even though I knew it was a pointless exercise, I rechecked my leather handbag where I usually kept them. Not there, I wondered where they could be?

The reason finding the keys was so important was because I was locked inside the house. My front door was one of those that you lock and unlock from the inside. Quite simply, I couldn't get out. I decided to phone Graham to ask him to come back and open the door. His mobile went straight over to voicemail so I left him a message. As I knew Graham would still be on his way to work, I couldn't phone his workplace just yet.

My next thought was for us to leave via the back garden. Sam and Connor got their bags together and as we passed through the kitchen, I grabbed the back-door key. At least that was in its place. We reached the towering wooden gate but as soon as we got there, I could see there was a problem. A huge one. The padlock was locked and I didn't have the key. Leaving the boys in the garden, I returned to the kitchen where all the keys were kept. Not one of them fitted the lock.

Hastily, we made our way back to the living room and it was then that I looked at the dependable clock. By this time, I was getting worried that the coach would leave without us. I tried to keep calm and stay in control. My next phone call was to the school office and I explained the situation to them. Searching everywhere, I had a strong feeling that Elizabeth had taken the keys but I kept looking anyway. They had disappeared as far as I was concerned. My greatest fear was that the keys would not come back in time and the children would miss the coach.

Next, I phoned Graham's workplace but he still hadn't arrived. I left them a message so they could pass it on to him, in case he hadn't listened to his voicemail. What else could I do? It was just a matter of time before the keys would come back. I asked Sam and Connor to look around the living room to see if they could spot them. They couldn't. Feeling helpless, I glanced back at the arm of the three-seater settee and there they were. My bunch of keys that I had left there in the first place. I was speechless.

That very minute, I unlocked the front door and we hurriedly made our way to the school. On arrival, I could feel everyone's eyes on us as we were the last ones to get to the crowded hall. Some members of staff were laughing and I presumed the lady from the office had told them what had happened. At least now, I could see the funny side of it too. It was farcical, but I did wonder if this practical joke had gone one step too far this time. I knew I hadn't misplaced the keys and was sure that Elizabeth had taken them. In the meantime, Graham had heard my voicemail and returned home.

On a more serious note, it did make me think that if there ever was a fire in the house, how would we escape? We couldn't even just hop over the back-garden fence or wall because they were too high. There was only one solution. The most sensible idea was to change the lock on the front door, which was something we did straightaway.

One afternoon, Graham had another encounter with Elizabeth. He was working alone at home doing some DIY, while myself and the children were visiting my nan. When the time came for him to collect us, he went to pick up his car keys but they weren't there. Certain he had placed them on the living room unit, he immediately thought Elizabeth must have taken them, so he decided to use my digital voice recorder. This is a handheld device that records sound, such as speech and other sounds, into a digital file that can be played back. It is easier to hear spirit by using one of these. He was hoping that Elizabeth would tell him where the lost keys were. Here is the actual dialogue at the time, which lasted forty-five seconds.

Slowly, Graham called out, "Is anybody here with me at the moment? If there is anybody here with me at the moment, can you tell me if you've moved my keys, because I put them by the front door on the unit, and now they're not there?" It remained silent. A further question followed. "So can you tell me where they are?" There was a long pause, as you must give spirit enough time to respond. Then Graham continued but this time he didn't ask a question. "I'm going to listen to this now and hopefully you've told me where the keys are."

When Graham played the recording back, this is what he heard. "Is anybody here with me at the moment? If there is anybody here with me at the moment, can you tell me if you've moved my keys, because I put them by the front door on the unit, and now they're not there?" At this point, to his amazement, there was an unmistakable giggle. It was unlike any child's laughter that he'd ever heard, although it was clearly coming from a young being. "I'm going to listen to this now and hopefully you've told me where the keys are."

It became apparent that Elizabeth had not revealed where the keys were, but she had made herself known in another way. She was playing one of her games and was finding it hilarious. Had Elizabeth put the keys in a different place for Graham to find? I wondered if she was engaging in a game of hide-and-seek.

The time came for Graham to try to find his keys. He walked over to the unit where he had originally left them, anticipating they would be there. Disappointedly, they hadn't returned. Feeling discouraged, Graham then scanned the room to see if they were elsewhere. Out of the corner of his eye, he noticed something gleaming in the sunlight that streamed in through the window. The keys. They had been left on the lid of the fish tank. Graham had sought and had eventually won the game.

I still have this recording on my digital voice recorder and it takes my breath away every time I listen to it. What's more, it gives me great pleasure to be able to share this with other people. My family and friends have been astonished by what they've heard. As time goes by, I hope that many other people will also get to hear it.

One of the most phenomenal experiences that I've ever had took place on a typical weekend afternoon. Graham had decided to remove a bamboo-framed mirror from the bathroom because it was looking worn and tired. It had belonged to the previous owner so it had been there before we moved into the house. As he released the mirror from the two hooks, he noticed a sizeable hole in the wall behind. That was unexpected! There was also an arch shaped mirror in the room, so he hadn't intended on replacing the mirror he'd just taken down. Thinking he'd have to fill the hole, he placed the mirror under his arm and took it downstairs to the outside rubbish bin. Graham then told me what he had found.

A little while later, I headed upstairs to use the bathroom. I went in through the door and turned around to inspect the hole. To my surprise, I could see that Graham had concealed it with another mirror. Instantly, I recognised it as one that his mum had given us a long time ago. We had tucked it away between my side of the bed and the unit and I'd forgotten it was there.

Rectangular in shape, its dimensions were 60 x 50cm. The ever so dusty glass was surrounded by an equally dusty frame. It was the darkest brown, with golden swirls that resembled leaves and berries. I wondered why Graham hadn't cleaned it, perhaps he hadn't got round to it. The mirror stared back at me, looking rightful in its place.

When I got back downstairs, I mentioned to Graham that I really liked the mirror and it would save him the job of filling the hole. In addition, I told him having two mirrors in the room would maximise the daylight. Confused, he shook his head. "I haven't put up a new mirror," he said.

"Well I haven't, so it must be you," I replied. I thought he was joking at first but then I realised he was deadly serious.

We stared at each other in utter disbelief but I knew he was thinking the same thing as me. It couldn't be, could it? If it wasn't us, then it must have been...it must have been Elizabeth. We were so shocked that we couldn't speak. She had moved and made good use of the mirror that had been consigned to oblivion. Incredibly, it must have taken a huge amount of energy to do that. As it stands, the mirror is still in the same place out of respect for Elizabeth.

I'm one of those people that has to have labels facing the right way round and by that, I mean the front. When I put my food shopping in the kitchen cupboards, I must have the tins, jars and packets exactly like this. It makes them look tidy and it's easier to see what the product is. The same applies to other rooms in the house, such as my bedroom, the living room and the bathroom. I like objects to be neatly and methodically arranged.

This is connected to an occurrence that came about in the bathroom. Having just got dressed for the day, I needed to clean my teeth. Leaving my bedroom, I walked across the landing, towards the bathroom. As I opened the decrepit door, I realised that something was different. Slowly, I looked around from left to right. To my complete horror, I could see that every single item had its label facing back to front. A feeling of dread enveloped me. I was uncomfortable. All I could think of was the fact it would take me ages to change everything around.

Conscientiously, I cast my mind back. Graham had gone to work and the children were at school. I had been the last person to use the bathroom and it certainly hadn't looked like this. It is my sincere belief that Elizabeth was trying to get a message across to me. She was telling me not to be so particular about how I position things. I'm sure Elizabeth wanted me to leave the items as they were but in the end I just had to turn them around. What I had experienced was not to be forgotten.

Incidentally, another event also became apparent in the bathroom. It was late in the evening and I had returned home from my nan's. Graham and I were about to relax with a drink or two. I felt like a refreshing can of cold lager so I opened the fridge and helped myself.

As I was about to sit down, I remembered I had some washing to put away. Reluctantly, I made my way upstairs with the folded clothes in my arms, the unopened can resting on top. In actual fact, I should have left it downstairs as there was no need to take it with me. I soon became worried that the can would topple over. As the bathroom was the nearest room to me, I placed it on the tiled shelf at the foot of the bath, before resuming my journey to the bedroom.

It didn't take long to put the clothes away and I was looking forward to having a drink. When I reached the bathroom, a spectacular sight beheld me. On the tiled shelf in front of me, was the can of lager and other products precariously stacked up high. There was the lager, shampoo, conditioner, shaving gel and perched at the very top, was a bottle of perfume standing on its lid. I had no idea how they were able to balance the way they did and not fall down.

When I moved them and tried to recreate the exact same thing, I couldn't do it.

No matter how hard I tried, it was impossible to balance everything how it was. The perfume would not stay upright on its lid by itself, let alone on the top of everything else. I couldn't understand how it had balanced in the first place because the lid was rounded! How Elizabeth did it, I don't suppose I'm ever meant to know.

At the time when Mia's baby teeth were falling out, she found great pleasure in chasing me around the house with the tooth in her open hand. Embarrassingly, I would run away screaming because I have a strong dislike for wobbly and lost teeth. I find it difficult to look at them and I most definitely couldn't bring myself to touch them. Strangely, I'm unsure why I've become panic-stricken as I don't recall any past trauma that might affect me.

It was dinnertime and I was hungrily devouring a slice of cheese and tomato pizza. I went to pick up the last piece, when my fingers brushed against something unexpected on the same plate. On inspection, to my disgust, I saw what was a molar tooth. Hysterical, I began shrieking and I recoiled back in fear. Mia had lost such a tooth the very same day but when I asked her if she had put it there, she promised she hadn't. I knew she was telling the truth. This had to be the work of Elizabeth but this time, I felt she had overstepped the mark.

Looking back, it still sends a shiver down my spine. Despite this, it could have been worse. Imagine if the tooth had been on the pizza and it had ended up in my mouth! It doesn't bear thinking about does it?

Chapter 8
Christmas Time

Christmas. It's that special time of year isn't it? A time for family and friends to be together. Spirits also like to be around their loved ones over the festive season. Elizabeth is no exception to this and understandably likes to make her presence known.

Every year, we like to put our decorations up on the 1st December. This is when it starts to feel really Christmassy to me. We have a six-foot artificial tree, which we place in the corner of the living room. I would love to have a real evergreen conifer, such as a pine tree, but unfortunately we can't because of our pets. Pine needles and dogs don't get along!

The dark green tree is decorated with gold, silver and purple baubles and has a golden star sitting on its very top branch. Glowing white lights adorn its shape. Sparkling tinsel is arranged above and around the canvas pictures. I like to keep it simple, yet effective. I'm not one for overdoing the decorations like some people do. The end result is a welcoming, cosy looking room.

Thankfully, it always makes me feel happier and warm inside, when the beautiful decorations are up. I become immersed in the spirit of Christmas. I'm sure other people experience this too. Mind you, Christmas isn't Christmas without the smallest, final touch. There is one decoration that always goes up last of all and sometimes we have to wait a little while for it to appear.

It is a fridge magnet, which sits quite rightly in its place on the fridge door. This magnet is unusual because it is in two parts. Each part has a magnet so you can push them together to make it whole. Oddly, it resembles some sort of green sea creature but I can't work out exactly what it is. Based on that, I named it the sea monster.

Each Christmas, once the tree has been decorated, the undivided sea monster becomes apparent, balancing on one of the bristly branches. Funnily enough, it is almost camouflaged because it is only a few shades lighter than the tree. It always makes me smile when I first see it, as it looks so out of place. Usually, it's the angel or star at the top of the tree that's the main decoration, but for us it's the sea monster! Often, it is moved from one branch to another so I have to find it again. This is the effort of Elizabeth and is evidently something she enjoys doing.

I love giving presents at Christmas and I aim to wrap them up well in some luxurious paper. By adding a glossy ribbon and a matching bow, it gives a splendid finish to the presentation. Don't get me wrong, I take great delight in receiving presents, but I still prefer to give them. I get pleasure in seeing the expressions on people's faces as they open them.

Christmas Eve is the time that I give Elizabeth her present. Lovingly, I leave it resting on one of the branches of the tree in the hope that she will collect it. Usually, it is a token gift but hopefully one she should have fun with. Over the last few years, I have also left a present for Boy, something that he can play with. I don't want him to miss out on the Christmas celebrations.

It's difficult enough to know what to buy a person for Christmas, let alone a spirit. As a spirit is made up of energy, there's no point in giving food as a gift. What would they do with it? Children here on Earth, more often than not, want the latest fad. In the run-up to Christmas, they are bombarded with toy advertisements in between their favourite programmes. Desiring products, some parents can't afford.

Growing up in the Victorian era, I assumed Elizabeth would prefer old-fashioned toys to play with. As it would be unrealistic to get hold of the original artefacts, I thought the next best thing was to look at modern day versions of the same. I really wanted to give Elizabeth something she could treasure, so I began thinking. To help me with ideas, I scoured the Internet.

Back in Victorian times, the toys were very expensive and the richer children would've had more to choose from. Only the wealthiest could afford a dappled grey rocking horse with a mane and tail made from real horsehair. They also had dolls houses with beautifully carved furniture, china or wax dolls, clockwork train sets, miniature soldiers, toyshops with toy food and intricate tea sets. Other popular items were: puppet theatres, jigsaw puzzles, alphabet bricks, skittle sets, sailing boats, Noah's Arks, kaleidoscopes, zoetropes and marbles made from real marble.

Poorer children would rarely have more than one toy and it was typically handed down through the generations or made by hand. Usually, they played with whatever they could find, such as climbing trees and lampposts or paddling in a brook. Often, the children would make their own toys, like cloth-peg dolls, paper windmills and skipping ropes. A tightly wadded piece of cloth would serve as a ball to kick around outside. In addition, a hobby horse could easily be made with a wooden pole. Sometimes, wheels would be attached to the base so it could be rolled around, rather than dragged along the ground. If they received pocket money, it was saved to buy spinning tops, ball and cups, hoop and sticks, pickup sticks, trapeze monkeys and other cheap wooden toys.

Books were enjoyed by Victorian children, rich or poor. They would read the same book over and over again. Some had charming, elaborate art on the covers. Others were in full colour or embossed with gold ink on cloth.

Thankfully, I now had many ideas of what to get Elizabeth so I decided to go shopping in Fareham to see what I could find. It wasn't difficult. The very first Christmas present I ever bought her was a little, fluffy, brown, toy dog.

Unsurprisingly, it looked cute with its big brown eyes and adorable face. I thought it would make the perfect gift for a seven-year-old girl, even if she was now in spirit.

Hiding the dog away at the top of my bedroom wardrobe, along with all the other Christmas presents, it remained there until Christmas Eve. It was then that I placed it on a beautifully decorated branch of the tree. This might sound strange but I didn't wrap the present, as I have always wondered if spirit is able to unwrap it. I wanted to keep it as simple as possible for Elizabeth to be able to have.

Christmas Day arrived. Excited like a child, I ran downstairs and opened the living room door. Peering in, I could see the dog had gone. I checked underneath the tree in case it had fallen during the night but it was nowhere to be seen. Feeling overwhelmed, I said out loud, "I hope you like your present, Elizabeth." She didn't knock but I knew she had heard me.

The following Christmas, I went shopping in Fareham once again and bought the ideal present for Elizabeth, from a well-known book retailer. They had a small section assigned to modern interpretations of old-fashioned children's toys and games. It was here that I discovered the brightly coloured, wooden spinner.

Measuring 6cm x 6cm, it was predominantly red with an orange border. In the centre, it had three different sized stars that were blue, yellow and orange. The long spindle was the colour of natural lightwood. It was certainly eye-catching and I thought Elizabeth would love to play with it.

I also spotted a spinner drum, more commonly known as a monkey drum. This is a small, musical instrument that has two beads attached to cord, which make a beating sound when it is turned from side to side. It was white, with a striking red and black pattern on the outside. As it is obviously a noisy toy, I wondered if Elizabeth would like this or not. I decided to buy it anyway but I had this niggling feeling that it wasn't quite right for her. If only I'd gone with my gut feeling.

Christmas morning soon came and I rushed downstairs to see if Elizabeth had taken her two presents. I was disappointed to find that the spinner and the spinner drum were still nestling between the branches of the ever-embracing tree. Sadly, I went to put the kettle on to make my usual morning cup of coffee before returning to the living room. When I next looked at the tree, to my absolute amazement I saw that the spinner had disappeared from its place although the spinner drum was still there. Elizabeth must have taken it in a matter of minutes. At that very moment, I knew that I have made the wrong decision in buying the spinner drum. I also knew that she would not come back for it later and that it would be left, unused, upon the tree.

At first, the living room looked so bare and cold. The decorations had come down and were packed away in their boxes, along with the lonely looking. All of the presents had been opened and put in their places, all except for one. The little spinner drum. I wasn't quite sure what to do with it, but after some thought, I decided to leave it on show a little longer. Carefully, I propped it up against the wall and it sat on top of the living room fire. Time passed but Elizabeth never did come for it, just as I had predicted.

The next Christmas present I bought Elizabeth was a pocket-sized bag of beautifully decorated glass marbles. About 1.5 cm in diameter, they had swirls of many colours throughout them. I knew that the Victorians loved to play marbles. Their favourite ones were made of real marble, but they were very expensive. Marbles made of glass were cheaper but the poorest children would have ones made of clay. I wondered if Elizabeth had ever owned any of these marbles. They were placed on the tree and by Christmas morning they had vanished.

One Christmas, I completely forgot to get a present for Elizabeth. It was Christmas Eve and I was sitting in the living room feeling pleased with myself about all the presents I'd chosen and wrapped. Then for some reason, I started to mentally list all the people I'd bought presents for.

It was then that I realised I'd forgotten to get Elizabeth anything. I gasped in disbelief. What was I to do? The shops were long shut and I had nothing to give her.

I racked my brain for inspiration and then I came up with an idea. Bingo! I would test out my creative skills and make Elizabeth something. There were some arts and crafts materials in the nearby cupboard, so I went to see what I could put together. Thoughtfully, I chose a plain coloured lollipop stick, some white pipe cleaners, pink felt, yellow wool, a stapler, scissors and several felt tips. This was all I needed in order for me to make my present.

Picking up the lollipop stick, I decided that it would form the basis of the stick doll. It was naturally the right colour so that was a good start. The white pipe cleaners made ideal arms as they were so flexible to work with. I twisted them into position, bending them at the elbow joints and then I stapled them to the body. Then I cut out an ankle-length gown from the pink felt and wrapped it around the lollipop stick, stapling it together. Next I snipped at the yellow wool so it resembled locks of hair and stapled them on. Finally, I conscientiously drew two large, blue eyes with long black lashes, a pink button nose and a full, red mouth. At last, my stick doll was complete.

I was thrilled with the outcome and I hoped Elizabeth would feel the same. Initially, I had felt terrible at not having bought her a present but now I didn't, because I has put much more of my time into making her something. Placing the doll on a branch of the tree, she looked illuminated by the twinkling lights that surrounded her. The very next morning, on Christmas Day, she had been taken away to her new home.

It was approaching Christmas and the time had come to begin buying presents.

Mia and her best friend, Caitlin, had been shopping in Gosport and she had come across the cutest looking teddy bear. She bought it there and then as a gift to Elizabeth from me. I felt it was very thoughtful of her and I was happy she had made just the right choice.

Standing at 17cm tall, the teddy bear was an unusual smoked salmon colour. It had dark eyes that peeked out from behind the fluffiness of its face and a sewn brown nose and mouth. The pads of its paws were cream with a pretty pink and green floral pattern. A matching bow, tied ever so neatly, covered its neck. So soft to the touch, it was crying out to be loved. This particular Christmas I had decided to buy Boy a present because he was Elizabeth's dog. I felt that he had missed out over the previous years.

That evening, I headed off to a well-known supermarket that sold dog toys. I was hoping to find something that was light in weight so it would balance on a branch of the tree. Rummaging around, I soon found a toy that made the perfect present. It was a fluffy, grey and black raccoon that squeaked when you pressed it. What dog doesn't like a squeaky toy? I set it aside with the teddy bear until it was Christmas Eve.

The time came for me to put the two presents on the tree. Although it wasn't too heavy, the teddy bear made the branch bow, but it didn't fall. Meanwhile, the dog toy sat on its branch with ease. Christmas Eve turned into Christmas Day and by the time I came downstairs, both the presents were gone. I wondered if Elizabeth had collected Boy's present or had Boy himself? Either way, I was delighted that they had been taken.

I was fortunate enough to win a thirty-minute one-to-one phone reading with a well-known British psychic medium. Therefore, I was over the moon when I found out, as I had been to two of her shows in the past, and had thoroughly enjoyed them. The competition was courtesy of a monthly spiritual magazine. As this person works well with photographs, I scanned over a photograph of myself and my two late granddads. I was hoping she could connect with them during the reading.

On the agreed date, she phoned me a little earlier than expected. She was just about to have her tea and asked if she could phone me straightaway afterwards. At the time, I was in the middle of cooking a full-blown roast dinner, so I had to down everything, and get my paper and pen ready to record the conversation. I could hardly wait.

By looking at my photograph, she was able to start the reading. I won't go into the whole conversation but I'll talk about some accurate information that I was given. She told me that I suffered from depression and that I had to take medication. Then she went on to say that I was punctual, a stickler for time. She also said that I wasn't one to talk about other people and that I keep things to myself. Furthermore, she asked if I was a teacher, as I like to help people get things right and that I was emphatic and would make a great counsellor.

Towards the end of the reading, she asked if there was anything I would like to ask her. I told her I had a spirit who communicates with me in my house and that she was called Elizabeth. At that very movement, she said she was going to say 'Lizzie', which was incredible, as I often call her Lizzie Beth. She continued by saying that Elizabeth was involved with the house and that she was about seven or eight years old. It's reassuring to know that she looks after me and loves me very much.

It was identified that there was paranormal activity in the kitchen and bathroom because they were a source of electricity and water. She also said I would often hear a *pop, pop, pop* sound. Perhaps she was referring to the popcorn which Elizabeth liked to play with. I found it interesting when she said that a boy of about fifteen years of age visits the house at Christmas time. He comes with Elizabeth from the 23rd to the 26th of December. Subsequently, I told her that I leave Elizabeth a Christmas present each year and she said that Elizabeth would like some blue ribbon for her hair.

I was asked if I'd won the reading through a competition and when I said yes, she said she would send me a goody bag. At the end of the reading, I wished her a great 2016 with her tour, and said that it had been lovely talking to her. She replied, "I haven't said this to anyone yet but Happy Christmas to you." In return, I wished her a happy Christmas too.

True to her word, in good time, a small package arrived full of goodies. There were two books she had written, a signed photograph, a named canvas shopping bag and some named badges. I felt so grateful for her kind gesture. She was such a genuine and down to earth person which I really appreciated.

About two months later, it would be Christmas and I knew exactly what present to buy Elizabeth. Nearer the time, Graham, Mia, Sam and I went shopping in Portsmouth, where I intended to find a shop that sold ribbon. It didn't take long for us to discover one and I made my way to the section I needed. I had a dilemma though. What shade of blue ribbon would she like most? Light blue, dark blue? I thought long and hard and then I envisaged Elizabeth with the palest blue ribbon in her long hair. The next decision was how much I needed so I decided to get one metre. That way, there would be enough there for her.

Before long, it was Christmas Eve. On this occasion, I had bought not only a present for Elizabeth and Boy, but also a small gift for the fifteen-year-old boy who visits at Christmas. In the past, I had put the presents on the branches of the tree but this year, I left the blue ribbon on the living room table. I thought it would be best to lay it out neatly. Alongside the ribbon was a tennis ball that I had bought for Boy and a mini construction kit for the visiting teenager.

When I awoke on Christmas morning, I was eager to see if the presents had been taken. At the speed of light, I made my way downstairs and opened the living room door. I fixed my gaze around the corner and waited with bated breath. All three presents were still there, positioned on the table.

Feeling disappointed, I carried on with the day; this very special day. Every now and then, I would glance over in the hope that the presents had disappeared. They hadn't. It wasn't until later in the morning, that I started to walk over to the table and noticed it was laid bare. The presents were gone. I felt ecstatic.

It was the October after that Christmas. Mia was in the living room when she wondered what our two dogs were playing with. On closer inspection, she saw a teddy bear and a raccoon dog toy. At this point, I came downstairs and to my astonishment, I recognised they were the very same presents I had given to Elizabeth and Boy two Christmases ago. I was confused as to why they had been returned. Was it because it was Mia's birthday and Elizabeth wanted her to have the teddy bear? The dogs were short of play things so did she want the dogs to have the dog toy? The dog toy has since vanished but I still have the teddy bear today.

Chapter 9
I Hear You

A question is a sentence worded so as to obtain information from a person but it this case it's from a spirit. The only difference, is that Elizabeth can only respond to closed-ended questions, which can be answered by a simple yes or no. I mentioned earlier in the book that Elizabeth communicates with me by knocking once for yes, or she'll remain silent for no. When she's finished answering questions or has to go, she knocks twice for goodbye.

There are many places that I ask Elizabeth questions but I find that I get the best responses when I'm in the kitchen. Nevertheless, I have had replies in the bathroom and living room, and on one occasion in Sam's bedroom. It can be during the day or the night. I think that some people assume you can only 'get hold' of spirits during the darkest hours. It doesn't matter if the room is a little noisy, although quiet is preferable as it is easier to hear her knocks. Either way she still makes herself known.

I usually have Graham with me, as I feel Elizabeth uses his energy to help her come through. He must have a strong energy about him, although I have had communication when I've been alone. Strangely, sometimes Graham can hear her knocks while other times he cannot. I on the other hand, am always able to hear them.

Each time Elizabeth comes forward, I am absolutely amazed and I feel so honoured that she has chosen me to communicate with. She can't always come through though, as her energy may be weak. One piece of advice I give to people is to always be respectful to spirit. This is something

I strive to be and I always thank Elizabeth at the end of a conversation. I have no reason to feel afraid of her and I appreciate the fact she takes the time to talk with me. Fortunately, I have asked Elizabeth many questions over the years and I would like to share some of them with you.

It was the afternoon and Graham and I were in Sam's bedroom, as he was fixing the door handle. I was talking to him about the fact we need to help ourselves if we want to get somewhere in life. Then I casually said, "Don't we, Elizabeth?" I wasn't expecting an answer but she suddenly started to knock very loudly in agreement. Surprised, I then went on to ask her if my book would be successful and she knocked once for yes.

At that moment in time, I had only just begun to write and I was finding it difficult to do. This reinforced what I had been talking about and gave me the inspiration and motivation to continue writing. On another occasion, I was painstakingly looking for some paperwork underneath the stairs, when Graham said, "That's a waste of time." Annoyed, I was about to question him, when I heard a really loud knock on the wooden floor in the adjoining dining room.

In an instance, I said, "Elizabeth, am I wasting my time?" Her distinct knock for yes could be heard once again. I went on to say, "I've found one piece of paper, is that all I will find?" She knocked once for yes to confirm what I had said. I then asked her if she was still there but there was no response and it remained silent.

Sometimes, Elizabeth will only be around for a fleeting moment. She had answered my questions and thought that was all I needed to know at the time.

Further communication took place late one night, while Graham and I were watching television in the living room. He was engrossed in a documentary about space and casually said, "Dad would like this programme." Graham's dad had sadly passed away a few years earlier. Straightaway, we heard a distinct knock for yes, next to the two-seater settee where Graham was sitting.

It was Elizabeth. I asked her, "Elizabeth, is Graham's dad here watching this?" Again, she clearly knocked once, near the dining room door.

I have the habit of changing the subject so I said, "Do you know we're trying to get fridge magnets for you?" She knocked once. I continued, "We will try and get them for you tomorrow in Fareham, would you like that?" This time, she knocked once but fainter. Realising she was fading, I asked, "Elizabeth, is your energy getting weaker?" I just about heard her knock once and then I asked, "Elizabeth, would you like to say goodbye?" It was then she knocked her signature twice for goodbye.

Many years back, I was invited to an evening at an 'acquaintance's' house, along with some other people. I say acquaintance because I only knew her to talk to at Sam's then football club. For confidentially reasons, I cannot name her. Even though she didn't know much about me, she seemed to take to me like a duck to water. I hadn't known her for very long and I had this uneasy feeling about her. Unfortunately, I couldn't quite put my finger on it but I believed she had ulterior motives. The problem was, I wasn't exactly sure what they were. Somehow, I seem to pick up on people's personalities and emotions.

When I arrived home after my evening out, I hoped Elizabeth would help answer some questions about her. I wanted to make sure I hadn't got the wrong end of the stick. Calling out, I asked, "Elizabeth, are you here?" It was silent. I asked again, "Elizabeth, if you're here, can you knock once?" Without hesitation, she knocked. Continuing, I asked, "Elizabeth, are you aware I went to my friend's house today?" She knocked once. "Is she a nice person?" She didn't respond. I carried on by saying, "Will she be a good friend to me?" It was silent. That silence told me everything I needed to know and I thanked Elizabeth. She acknowledged this by knocking twice to say goodbye.

I had been right. Not wanting to appear rude, I still said hello to her at the football club but I distanced myself. That way, I wouldn't become too involved with her and judging by Elizabeth's advice, it was the best thing to do. Luckily, she never did invite me out again, which is just as well.

Another time, I had the miserable experience of falling over an empty laundry basket while sorting out the clothes. I knew immediately that I had hurt my wrist but I wasn't sure whether I needed to go to the doctors or not. On the whole, I don't tend to go unless I really have to. Earlier that morning, my watch strap had come undone, so I removed my watch and put it to one side. To be honest, I forgot all about it.

The day passed quickly and I still hadn't contacted the doctors. Graham returned home from work and placed his keys on top of the wooden bookcase. It was then that he became aware of my watch nearby. He asked me why I wasn't wearing it so I explained what had happened. I wondered if Elizabeth had made the watch strap come undone intentionally because she knew I was going to fall. Perhaps she didn't want me to injure my wrist any more than I already had.

Before long, we made our way to the kitchen. I had some questions that I hoped Elizabeth would answer. Speaking softly but clearly, I asked, "Elizabeth, are you here?" There was no reply. I repeated, "Elizabeth, are you here?" It was then that I heard her knock once for yes. Feeling thankful, I continued. "Hello Elizabeth, do you know that I fell over today?" She knocked once. I then asked, "Is that why you made my watch come undone?" The knock was loud.

Wanting her guidance, I asked, "Do I need to see a doctor about my wrist?" It remained silent. As luck would have it, I didn't need to make an appointment. I always followed Elizabeth's advice as it was accurate. Cheerfully, I put my last question to her, which was unrelated to what we had been talking about. "Are you happy that I'm feeling happier?" she replied with a knock. This made me smile, as I had been feeling down for a while but was now thinking in a more positive mood. Evidently, Elizabeth had recognised this. I then ended the short conversation by saying, "Goodbye Elizabeth, and thank you."

On another occasion, there had been some activity over the last two days and I felt I needed Elizabeth to validate it was her. As I asked a lot of questions, I will set them out as follows:

I began. "Elizabeth, are you here?"

Without delay, there was a knock for yes.

"Did you spell 'take care of Dad' with the fridge magnets yesterday?"

Yes.

"Do you think of Graham as your daddy, here in the living world?"

Yes.

"Is Graham feeling sad?"

Yes.

"Graham feels he doesn't need looking after, is he wrong?"

Yes.

"Did you place the spinner on my paperwork last night?"

Yes.

"Did you place the spinner in the bathroom tonight?"

Yes.

"Did you see Sam's friend here at the house today?"

Yes.

"Do you think he's a nice boy?"

This time it remained silent for no.

"Is he unhappy?"

Yes.

"Is his mother a bad person?"

Yes.

"Did you see her in our house this evening?"

Yes.

Then Elizabeth suddenly knocked twice for goodbye.

I now had the confirmation that I needed. Elizabeth had also answered questions about people that I intuitively knew the answers to beforehand. As I mentioned earlier, I often get these 'feelings' about people. Maybe I'm more of an empath than what I realise.

A different communication took place on Mia's eighth birthday and once again activity had taken place. I felt I needed to speak to Elizabeth about it.

I began. "Elizabeth, are you here?"

There was an instant knock for yes.

"Are you aware it is Mia's eighth birthday today?"

Yes.

"Do you like her birthday cards?"

Yes.

"Were you with us when my brother and his family came to visit today?"

Yes. "Do you like them?"

Yes.

"Do you like nice children visiting the house?"

Yes.

"Did you think we had lots of fun?"

Yes.

"Did you know that Fiona was scared?"

Yes.

Graham said he had heard laughter, so I questioned Elizabeth about it.

"Were you laughing at the bottom of the stairs because you found it funny?"

Yes.

"Were you near my brother today?"

Yes.

"Did you come with us when we went to the Isle of Wight on Sunday?"

This time it remained silent for no.

"Did you think we all had a good time?"

Yes.

"Have you drained Graham's camera batteries to give you energy?"

Yes.

"Did you leave the second spinner on the banister post by the bathroom?"

Yes.

"Did you put the spinner in my handbag?"

Yes.

"Did you also put the spinner underneath me, when I was asleep on the settee?"

Yes.

"Did you turn my mobile phone off?"

Yes.

"Did you make a birthday card fall on the floor today?"

Yes.

At this point, Elizabeth knocked twice for goodbye.

Once again, Elizabeth had answered all of the questions that I put to her. It does take a lot of their energy, and not all spirits are able to do it. Despite the fact that she is only seven, I feel Elizabeth is a much-evolved spirit. She is wise beyond her years as she has the wisdom of someone with an old soul.

The time came for our next communication and I asked Elizabeth some questions about events that had taken place.

I began. "Elizabeth, are you here with me?"

She knocked once for yes.

"Did you throw the spinner just now?"

Yes.

"Did you put the spinner on top of the children's nightclothes today?"

Yes.

"Did you put the rubber duck on top of my mobile phone?"

Yes.

"Have you seen the ornaments Mia brought home from the party today?"

Yes.

"Do you like them?"

Yes.

"Which is your favourite ornament, the frog?"

This time it remained silent for no.

"Is it the chicken?"

Yes.

"Have you seen the magic set Mia brought home?"

Yes.

"Do you like the magic set?"

Yes.

"Did you get the popcorn from the kitchen cupboard?"

No.

"Have you been collecting the popcorn the children have dropped?"

Yes.

"Do you think it's a fun game?"

Yes.

I then asked Elizabeth if she could throw some popcorn near me. Almost immediately, a kernel brushed against my ankle.

"Thank you for doing that Elizabeth. Did you like Mia playing the popcorn game with you?"

Yes.

"Did you make the popcorn land in my lap earlier?"

Yes.

"Did you also put popcorn in my hair?"

Yes.

Elizabeth then knocked twice for goodbye.

I was delighted that Elizabeth had responded to my questions and I felt uplifted. It doesn't matter how many times she communicates with me, it's always as wondrous as the first time it happened. Sometimes we have a very short conversation, while other times we have longer ones. Quite often, I say to Graham that I need to get hold of Elizabeth, as though it is as straightforward as calling someone up on the phone.

On a further occasion, I was visiting my nan, when my ruby cross necklace fell from around my neck. The clasp wasn't loose so I couldn't understand how it had happened. When I returned home that evening, I decided to ask Elizabeth's some questions so I could get to the bottom of it. I called out and asked, "Elizabeth, are you here?"

She replied with a knock.

"Did you make my necklace fall off at Nan's?"

Her knock was unmistakable.

I continued, "Was it Granddad…?"

Astonishingly, she knocked 'yes' before I could finish the sentence. I was about to say, "Was it Granddad giving me a sign?" Then I asked her, "Is that because he was unable to do it himself?"

There was another knock.

My final question to Elizabeth was, "Is he watching down on us?"

She knocked again.

I felt reassured. It was comforting to know, as my granddad had passed away only one month earlier. Usually it takes spirits some time to learn how to channel their energy after they've passed over so this may have been the case for my granddad. What I do know, is that Elizabeth will always speak the truth and this has helped me in so many different ways.

Chapter 10
Darker Forces

Where there is light, there is dark. There is strong and there is weak. Where there is lovingness there is hatefulness. There is positivity and there is negativity. All of these opposites can be found in the spirit realm.

Elizabeth is a good soul who has a positive energy. She has a high frequency, which is associated with the light. White light is the purest light and is the space within the spirit realm that encompasses positive energies. It can be called upon for assistance, healing and to offer protection from negative energies. However, it cannot be used to harm anyone or anything and it cannot be harmed in any way. If you saw a white mist as opposed to a black mist, it is a marvellous sign. It may be that you notice just a spark of white light, or it could be a full-bodied shadowy figure flooded in sparks of white light.

In comparison, there are bad souls who have a negative energy. They have a low frequency connected with the dark. Negative spirits were most likely negative people in their time on earth. Like a very selfish and uncaring person, negative spirits are also very selfish and don't care about the harm or damage they can create. There ultimate desire is to have power and control over people. Therefore, sometimes, a negative spirit will seek to link to the physical body or aura to cause harm. Subsequently, this can affect that person emotionally, physically and spiritually in what they think, feel, say, do and desire. It gives the negative spirit a chance to do human things again. This process is known as a psychic attack.

Negative energies can be picked up almost anywhere where negative people, emotions or thoughts exist, and they can build up in your own home. Unwelcome human emotions and actions are the main cause of negativity. Any type of self-defeating emotion or thought such as defeatism, envy, anger and violence can accumulate in the atmosphere. Prolonged states of rage, discontentment, vindictiveness and many kinds of fears can entice these negative energies. When things happen in our lives it is common to feel angry or fearful but these occurrences can generate conditions that set up the energetic attraction.

Violence, in all its forms, whether physical, mental or emotional is a very powerful lure for negative and dark forms of energies. The same can be said for the regular use of alcohol, drugs and cigarettes. When we become drunk from alcohol or drugs our auras become significantly weakened and negative energies are attracted to the energy set up by these conditions.

Unfortunately, I have had some experiences associated with negative spirits that I hope will never repeat themselves again. It invoked this feeling of dread inside me each time it happened. I always called upon Elizabeth, asking her to help protect me. As I see it, she would always do her upmost to keep me safe.

On one occasion, I was getting myself ready to go to work. I was in the living room putting on my make-up, when I heard an almighty crashing noise coming from the kitchen. Knowing there was nobody in there, I wondered what on earth was going on so I rushed to see what had caused it. I was soon joined by Mia, who had also heard the loud sound from where she was sitting in the dining room.

Slowly, I looked around the kitchen but there was nothing to be seen. All of a sudden, I saw what appeared to be a thick, black mist. It was coming from the gas oven and it was flowing down like a waterfall towards the laminate floor. As I stared in amazement, I could see what I can only describe as those frozen ready-made meal trays, falling headlong, in between the engulfing mist. Mia, who was standing next to me also witnessed the phenomenon taking place. It was terrifying, yet breath-taking to watch.

In next to no time, it stopped. My eyes surveyed the floor area but there was absolutely nothing there, not a single tray in sight. I didn't have any of these trays in the house so I was completely baffled as to what I had seen. What I do believe, is that the blackness represented negative energy, unlike Elizabeth who is surrounded by white light and represents positive energy.

There was a time, when Graham and I were going through a rough patch as most couples do. Therefore, there were a lot of negative feelings between us and tension in the air. Graham, myself and the children had spent the afternoon round my nan's house and had returned home in the early evening. As I opened the front door, I immediately detected the distinct smell of smoke, as though something was burning. Panic-stricken, my first thought was to race to the kitchen to see if there was a fire.

I dropped my two bags onto the porch floor and made my way through the living room, like an arrow from a bow. On arrival, there was nothing burning and no smoke to be seen. Me being me, I was always so careful about checking that appliances and electrical sockets had been turned off, before I left the house. Upstairs, it had to be upstairs. I quickly opened the door at the bottom of the stairs and it was then that the powerful smell hit me. At this point, I knew it must be coming from above.

Running up the stairs, the smell led me to my bedroom. I looked around but there was nothing on fire. Wanting to be on the safe side, I swiftly checked the other two bedrooms and then the bathroom, before returning to my bedroom. Relieved, I thanked my lucky stars nothing was burning. Still, I needed to find out what had caught on fire because clearly something had. Meticulously, I checked for the obvious signs to see if anything was black or if there were ashes anywhere.

As I started to go through my personal belongings, to my complete shock, I noticed that a box of mahogany hair dye had been badly burnt. It was blackened from the base of the packet to three quarters of the way up. There were ashes surrounding it. This really alarmed me because I then knew it was the work of a spirit, a bad one. There was no other way that the box could have caught alight. I knew it wasn't Elizabeth and I believe that a negative spirit had been feeding off of all the negative feelings that Graham and I had created. We had attracted a dark energy into our home.

All sorts of questions raced through my mind. What if the house had caught fire? Everyone knows how easily cardboard burns, it wouldn't have taken much for the wooden shelf to have gone up in flames. I couldn't comprehend how this had happened in my own home, a place where my children should feel safe. My next fear was that this could happen again but on a much bigger scale. What if there was a fire while we were sleeping or while we were out and it escalated into something much worse? Would we have to move house? Would the negative spirit follow us?

After I had some time to collect my thoughts, I became more rational. I explained to Graham that we would have to work at getting along and to think positively, so that the negative spirit would weaken and go away. Although, to be honest, I didn't know if it would leave that easily. We agreed to give things a go and gradually over the next few days, we repaired any damage between us that had been done and soon our relationship became harmonious.

Fortunately, we never did experience another fire but it could have certainly happened again. The time came for me to call upon Elizabeth and she confirmed that a negative spirit had been in the house. By changing the way Graham and I thought and behaved, it had not been strong enough to stay. To say I was relieved was an understatement.

On another occasion, it was Graham who experienced the paranormal activity. Being a weekday morning, I was at work but Graham had booked the day off, and was relaxing at home. It began with a single, loud knock at the front door. Graham didn't want to answer because he wasn't expecting anyone, and he thought it was probably a sales rep ready to pitch their sale. Whoever it was, was insistent and knocked hard again. Annoyed, Graham chose to ignore it and carried on watching television. Suddenly, there was an intimidating *'knock, knock, knock'*. This time, Graham wondered what the urgency was so he walked over to the porch, and proceeded to open the front door.

He was greeted by a man, a stranger, someone he could not recollect. As his gaze fell upon the stranger's face, the man asked, "Is Shella there?"

Graham answered, "Shella's at work but do you want to leave your number, so she can get back to you?"

The man replied, "No."

Then Graham asked, "Who shall I say called?"

The man then said, "It doesn't matter, goodbye." and he slowly walked away.

I arrived home at lunchtime, as I always do, and Graham explained what had happened. Curiously, I asked him what the man looked like. He described him in detail, from the cut and colour of his hair down to his build and the clothes he was wearing. I thought long and hard back to my past but nobody of this description came to mind. This was someone I didn't recognise. It couldn't have been that important if he hadn't left his name or number but I still wondered who it could have been.

Graham went on to explain that the man was very aloof and wouldn't give anything away about himself. I thought this was very odd. If I wanted to get hold of someone, I would certainly leave my details if someone else answered the door. Why wouldn't I?

Later that day, I called upon Elizabeth to see if she could shed any light as to who this mystery man was. I began, "Elizabeth, are you here with me?" It was quiet. I continued. "Elizabeth, can you hear me?" Instantly, there was a knock for yes but it was somewhat faint. Despite this, I knew it was her. Then I asked her, "Elizabeth is your energy weak?" She knocked once again, still as faint as before. Feeling disappointed that she might fade away before I could finish asking my questions, I asked with all possible haste, "Elizabeth, do I know the man who knocked at the door today?" There was silence. I had this thought at the back of my mind that I couldn't push away so I asked, "Elizabeth, was it a negative spirit that called here?" She knocked quietly and then knocked twice for goodbye.

At this point, I could hardly get my head around the fact that a spirit had knocked on my front door asking to speak to me. Graham confirmed that the spirit had appeared as a full-bodied, solid human form and there was nothing about the spirit that would make him think otherwise. I desperately wanted some more answers but I knew that Elizabeth's energy was low. She needed to be stronger.

Regrettably, I'd have to leave it until the following evening. The next day arrived and soon it was time to call upon her again. "Elizabeth, can you be here please?" She knocked strongly. "Elizabeth, does the negative spirit mean me harm?" I heard a knock. "Did he need to be invited into the house to cause harm?" There was another knock. Thankfully, Graham had not invited him to come into our home. I still had some questions I wanted to ask. "Elizabeth, does he still want to come in?" It remained silent. I felt slightly relieved by this time. "Did he go by himself?" It was quiet. "Elizabeth, did you get rid of him?" There was no answer. This left me feeling rather confused. I then asked, "Did somebody help you get rid of him?" A distinct knock could be heard. I wondered, could it be someone in spirit that I knew?

The closest family member who had passed over was Graham's dad, so I put the question to Elizabeth. "Did Graham's dad help you to get rid of the negative spirit?" She knocked a resounding yes. I was amazed. They had joined forces to create a stronger energy to drive away this bad soul, who clearly wanted to bring himself into our home. I imagined that he must have been a very negative energy as it took two positive energies to banish him. That would explain why Elizabeth's energy was weak the day before.

What is clear is that spirits work together in the spirit realm just as humans do here on earth. I wondered if it was the same negative spirit that had burnt my box of hair dye. He must have been very powerful to have taken the form of a human being and be able to have a normal conversation with Graham. At the time, when Graham first told me that a man had called for me, I was half expecting him to come back. Obviously, he never did for reasons I now understand. This is one experience that I often think about and marvel over.

At the age of eight, Mia encountered what is known as a shadow person. Shadow people are different to positive spirits in that they are dark in colour. It is the perception of a patch of black shadow, darker than the surrounding night, that appears and behaves as a living, human figure. They are generally male in appearance. Facial features, clothes and other details are usually completely undetectable because of the absence of light. This phenomenon can also be described as a black mass. A number of religions, legends and belief systems describe shadow people as shades of the lower realm.

Seeing a shadow person face to face is more unusual, as they are more commonly seen in and out of peripheral vision. If seen in direct vision, it seems that shadow people are seen alone. Their movement can be regular human movement or it can be faster, slower or more irregular than an average person's gait. It is even possible to look away from and look back at them without a change in their presence or appearance. They are aware of us and react to us watching them. Generally, they retreat when noticed and disappear around corners, or go through a solid wall.

Shadow people rarely speak or try to communicate with us and they are mostly found in homes, very often in bedrooms. Often, they tend to remain hidden as if in wait for someone. They are becoming an increasing area of study for many people and there have been countless reports connected to shadow people. Obviously, many people try to link seeing such beings to some sort of mental or emotional issue or relating to having sleep disorders or lack of sleep. Others, blame overactive imaginations.

When Mia became first became aware of the shadow person, she was in the bathroom having just washed her hands. Mia wasn't tired and it wasn't early in the morning or just before bedtime. One of the most interesting things about it, was that the experience took place during the day. It began when she looked towards her bedroom which was opposite the bathroom.

We heard a scream and Graham and I ran upstairs as fast as we could. Mia was standing in the bathroom, inconsolable. As you can imagine, it took some time to get her to explain what exactly had happened. When she was able to, she told me what she had seen. It was a dark, male figure pacing across her bedroom, a number of times. He then sat down on Mia's bed with his back to her, then turned around to look at her, then proceeded to face the other way and look out of the window. I gently asked her, "Was the man taller than Daddy?"

She replied, "He was about the same height." So that would make him about six foot tall.

I then said, "What clothes was he wearing?"

Her answer was, "He wasn't wearing any clothes."

I continued. "Did you see his face?"

Mia replied, "He didn't have a face." Then I went on to ascertain that he hadn't tried to communicate with her and he hadn't walked through any physical objects in the bedroom.

Even though Mia was quite young at the time, she still remembers the experience to this day. She can still give me the same description as before but in a more adult way. It did worry her for a long while and it took some time before she would sleep in her own room again. I therefore, sincerely believe that shadow people walk amongst us.

Chapter 11
In Search of Spirit

In the past, I have been to a number of paranormal investigations. This entailed me investigating both public and private locations, that were reported to be haunted by ghosts or had spirit activity. The desired outcome was to gather evidence to support the existence of paranormal activity. Often, this was achieved.

I say 'ghosts' and 'spirit' because I believe they are very different to each other. Seldom, do I use the word ghost because my predominant interest is in spirit, which is the form Elizabeth has taken. My interpretation of a ghost, is a person that chose not to go into the white light as they had a valid reason to stay behind, and consequently became a disembodied soul. Sightings of ghosts are known as 'residual energy' and this is where an emotional episode is replayed over and over again at the same place and time. Ghosts cannot communicate with us.

A spirit on the other hand, is an intelligent soul who is able to communicate with the living. It is a person that chose to follow the white light to the other side. Spirits are not restricted to one place and are able to move from one dimension to another. They can return to us at free will in 'visitation'. This is why I refer to Elizabeth as a spirit in my writing.

Many of the paranormal investigations took place at a well-established naval museum, situated in a historic setting in Gosport. In addition to the main museum, there were several outbuildings that I was able to investigate. These sessions were led by two, experienced paranormal investigators who I warmed to as soon as we met. Typically, we would begin at 8pm and end at 2am.

As we both have an interest in the paranormal, Graham and I attended together. Depending on the time of year, we had to think carefully about what clothes we needed to wear. It was best to be suitably dressed for the weather conditions or it could make for an uncomfortable night.

In the middle of winter, I would wrap up warm in jeans, a couple of thin-layered tops, a woollen jumper and a thick, waterproof coat. A matching scarf, hat and gloves would also be favoured. My feet would be covered in two pairs of ankle socks and low-heeled boots that have an adequate grip. Sensible footwear is always important, especially if you're visiting outbuildings or other outside locations, as the ground can be very uneven and there may be steep, winding steps. Furthermore, if it's rained or raining at the time, it makes it very slippery underfoot.

During the summer months, I would wear combats and a loose-fitting t-shirt because they are comfortable but cooling at the same time. I would also take a lightweight fleece or hoodie with me, as it often turns that much colder as the night progresses. In Britain, our evenings outside are renown for being chilly, even in the middle of July! My footwear would be a pair of cotton, trainer socks and breathable trainers, as they would still protect my feet but help stop them from overheating.

The next matter we had to consider was what equipment we needed to take with us. First and foremost, a torch with a powerful beam was an essential item so we could navigate our way around, when darkness fell. Sometimes, we had to walk single file up and down flights of deteriorating stairs and through long, narrow corridors, so it was always worth taking a torch each. Secondly, a mobile phone was important because we then had access to a telephone, in the event of an emergency. It also allowed us to take pictures and record videos. What's more, it could be used as a backup torch if required.

Time and again, a pocket-sized notepad and a couple of pens came in handy for jotting down key information. I always carried a spare pen in case the other one ran out. Although I endeavoured to record paranormal activity as it occurred, this was not always possible, so I would document it immediately afterwards. Usually, under torchlight, I'd write down where it took place, when it came about, what happened and who was involved. It was worthwhile, as we might have forgotten the details by the time morning came.

Spare batteries. We always brought enough for our torches and other paraphernalia. To be able to communicate with us, spirits need a lot of energy so they have to accumulate it from somewhere. It is theorised that they can use the energy from the batteries in our devices. This drain can cause equipment to stop working as there is an instantaneous loss of battery charge. For that reason, it was always in our best interest that we had plenty of extra batteries.

Amongst the other equipment that we chose to take was the Spirit Box, which I have touched on before. This modified portable AM/FM radio quickly and continually scans the radio stations. Its purpose, is to pick up the voices or sounds of spirits. As it happens, the Spirit Box is my preferred choice of communication because it has given me many accurate answers.

Another tool that I found useful was a pendulum. This is made up of a reasonably long chain, about six inches in length, with a weight on the end. Mine is an amethyst, which is a purple, translucent, semi-precious stone. Its colour represents the spirit and spirituality. Amethyst promotes spiritual protection and purification, intuition, peace and calm balance.

Using a pendulum is straightforward, if used correctly. The aim is to communicate with spirit and your spirit guide works through the pendulum. It can help people work out answers to all kinds of questions. I've used it to find lost items before.

Holding it in my dominant hand, I would loop the chain over my index finger. The end of the chain would be between my thumb and index finger with the pendulum swinging freely. Quietly, I would then ask my spirit guide to communicate with me using the stone. I would ask them to show me yes and wait for the response. Usually, it will move a certain way. I would then ask them to show me no and wait for it to move in a different way. When you get the answers to how you receive yes and no, the process of using a pendulum can begin. The pendulum should stop swinging when I ask it to. It is then that I can question and wait for an answer. I find that using the pendulum is a reliable way to connect with spirit.

An additional device that I particularly like is the EMF meter. Therefore, this went along with us on our investigations. It is an abbreviation of electromagnetic fields. I make use of the EMF meter because it is theorised that a ghosts or spirits presence, can be detected with a fluctuation in temperature and electromagnetic energy in the area.

If spiritual activity has taken place in the appointed frequency range, the meter response reflects this. The meter works off an inductor, which senses an alternating magnetic field and this generates a small voltage. Subsequently, this voltage is then amplified and used to give an output measurement. I have a digital EMF meter so if there is no EMF present, the lights will remain unlit and there will be a '0' on the indicator. When EMF is present, the lights will be lit and there will be a higher number on the indicator. A little or considerable amount of EMF will show on the meter.

As all of the investigations took place during the darker hours, another piece of equipment that came in useful was a night vision camera. This has a built-in infrared light for recording images in the darkest dark. It captures the necessary evidence by using the infrared to enhance the image. There is a built-in hard drive so the footage is easily uploaded to a computer to analyse the findings. In my view, a video record of what happened is always an excellent idea in case you missed something with the naked eye, which is very likely in the black of night. Just because we can't see it, it doesn't mean it's not there.

A further gadget that we had a liking for was a digital dictaphone, which is essentially a voice recorder. It is a method of recording and editing the spoken word in real time. Voices become digitally recorded on the internal memory inside the recorder, which can then be uploaded to sound files to our computer so we analyse, enhance and save them. Furthermore, it is straightforward to use with record, stop, rewind, fast forward and erase at the touch of a button. Known as electronic voice phenomenon or EVP, it offers some of the most compelling evidence of spirits. EVP are sounds found on electronic recordings that are understood to be the voice of spirits that have been either unintentionally recorded or intentionally asked for and recorded.

One other item that we always packed was our laser pen, which is a small, high-powered, handheld device. This fills the room with vibrant, green laser dots that create a grid like pattern, which is used for detecting motion or shadow during an investigation. Spectacularly, the dots scatter across the floor, walls and ceiling so if anything moves in front of the laser, you will see a displacement or inconsistency in the grid. They are great for catching potential proof when used in front of recording equipment. Green laser light is preferable to red, as it disperses more in the air, which makes the laser beam highly visible in the darkness. Also, the size and shape of the dots can be changed by turning the adjustable lens.

Finally, the last instrument we needed to take with us was our voice. I feel that spirits want to communicate with the living so they will try to when given the opportunity. The technique that we used was 'calling out'. It's so important to be patient when doing this. To begin the session, I always ask for psychic protection. I then ask a series of questions and then wait several seconds to give the spirit time to respond. Always begin with imperative questions to open the lines of communication and ask ones that can be answered with a simple 'yes' or 'no'. This is an example of how I would conduct a session and the questions I would ask them.

"I'm calling all positive spirits to come forward and make their presence known, and to protect me from any negative spirits."

"Are there any spirits here with me?"

"How many spirits are there?"

"Are you a male spirit?"

Wanting to find out their first name, I begin at the letter 'A' and slowly go through the alphabet. I then go through the same process to find out the second letter of their name. Following this, I call out various names until I discover who I am communicating with.

"When were you born?" I would state a year that I thought was relevant and take it from there.

"How old were you when you passed over?" I would say certain ages.

"What claimed your life?" I would express different circumstances.

"Did you work here?" You might want to establish exactly what job they did.

"Did you enjoy your work here?"

"Where do you most like to visit?" I would name areas in close proximity.

Interested to find out about their family I would ask

"Are you married?"

Depending on the answer I would then ask

"Is he/she in spirit?"

"Do you have any children?"

If the answer is yes I would ask

"Are they in spirit?"

I would then put forward

"Can you confirm what year it is?" I would then list some different years.

I would finish with

"Will you stay with me as I move around the buildings?"

At this point, I would end the session by thanking the spirit for speaking to me. Politely, I would then ask the energy to return to the spirit realm. I am always in awe of any communication that I receive and I spend a few moments reflecting upon what I have heard. This is very special to me and I feel so blessed.

Pre write your questions as you may well forget some important ones, especially if you get through to someone and in surprise, your mind goes blank. Bear in mind a spirit may not have enough energy to answer them all so put the fundamental ones first. On all occasions, give spirit plenty of time to respond to each question. Above all, be respectful. Remember, you can only get yes or no answers so it may be best to keep the questions simple, as I do. If you are using a spirit box you can ask more detailed questions. By using a recording device, it may present actual words when you listen back, that you didn't hear at the time. I would always recommend doing this.

Another method we used was a *séance*. It is a meeting at which people endeavour to communicate with spirit. This practice has lasted the test of time and is still used nowadays. The word '*séance*' is French and means seat, sitting or session.

All you need to conduct a *séance* is the presence of obliging sitters who are of the right mind-set and intention. It is essential to have an embracing atmosphere and the most basic requirement is an open mind to all possibilities of who you might hear from. Thoughtfully, we would stand, rather than sit, in a circle and hold hands with the people next to us. Everyone would then focus their attention. The purpose of the circle was to create an area of energy that could attract spirit. It is preferable to have a large group, as this can generate more energy than a smaller one. Our circle would usually consist of at least twelve people or so. By linking hands, this allows the energy to flow through each person. You must not let go of each other's hands until the session has been closed down because you will lose all of the energy that has been summoned.

One of the experienced paranormal investigators would be the facilitator and lead the group using their energy. That person would then ask the spirit to provide a sign of its presence. If the spirit is present, they would politely invite them to answer some questions. Once the *séance* is underway, members of the group can also ask questions. Responses are often in the form of knocks although other sounds might be heard.

We would also request the spirit to use our energy to slowly raise our arms into the air. If they were lifted up, we then ask them to gently lower them back down to their normal position. Sometimes, our arms wouldn't move or move only a little but occasionally they would end up way above our heads. The sessions would last anywhere from twenty minutes to forty minutes or longer. Often, the ending of the *séance* occurs naturally when the spirit energy in the room dissipates. After we have finished, we always thank spirit for being with us.

Occasionally, we would participate in a table-tipping session. This is a form of *séance* in which several people sit around a table and gently place their hands on its edges. With their hands resting, the experienced paranormal investigator would then lead the session by asking questions and wait for spirit to move the table in response. If this was successful, there would be rapping and knocking noises on the table but as it continues, the table would vibrate and eventually begin to move. The table could go backwards and forwards or move in a circular motion, as well as performing other movements. Incredibly, it is even possible for the table to rise in the air although I have never experienced this.

Our group would consist of about five to six people, I would suggest having at least four. A considerable number of sitters will increase the energy that is required to move the table. We would use a small, wooden table that could sit everyone comfortably. It is best to avoid using a table that is too large or heavy. Each person's hands should be on the table at all times and they need to be as still as possible. Respectively, we would ask simple questions that require a yes or no answer. By waiting patiently in between questions, it gives spirit time to respond.

In reflection, we could have asked more detailed questions by slowly reciting the alphabet and waiting for sprit to spell out words and sentences, but this takes up a lot of time. Unfortunately, we sat through a number of uneventful sessions before any activity occurred. When it did take place, we heard knocks on the table and it moved repeatedly from side to side. It was amazing to have witnessed such a moment.

As part of the investigations, we would use glass divination as a way of communicating with spirit. This can establish whether spirit is present to make contact with us, by them moving a glass across a table. Spirit can use our energy to communicate yes or no answers to questions asked by a group of people. We would use the same smooth table as we did for the table-tipping session and have a relatively light glass. This glass would be placed in the middle of the table with a pye or 'no' indicator placed at the opposite ends. Our indicators were a bright white light and a brilliant red light. The group would be made up of about four to six people and we would make sure there was plenty of space for us to stand around the table. Then, the colour relevance of the lights would be made clear to spirit. Each person would then place their right index finger on the upturned glass, without using any pressure.

After asking for protection, we introduced ourselves and asked spirit to communicate by moving the glass. As always, spirit is requested to move the glass by using the collective energy of the group and reply by moving the glass to the 'yes' or 'no' indicators. Then the traditional method of calling out questions would take place. Frequently, the glass would then move as the energy built up, sometimes quite vigorously in circles around the table. Often, questions put to spirit are answered by the glass moving to a particular person they may wish to make contact with. It is fortunate that we have been very successful in achieving a lot of movement in response to our questions. The sessions usually lasted between twenty to thirty minutes but these sittings can last for quite some time depending upon the amount of activity experienced. We would then close the session down by thanking spirit for talking with us.

Dowsing rods have been in use for centuries as a tool to detect underground water, minerals and ley lines but they can also be used to find lost items, or they can be used for divination and asking questions to spirit. Usually, we would use these on our investigations to identify any areas of paranormal activity. The theory is that the rods act as a transmitter of hidden energy sources in its many forms and that spirit reside within these fields, drawing upon the energy to make themselves apparent. This means they can respond to yes and no questions that we put forward to them.

Whilst the old-fashioned dowsing rods appeared as a wooden forked stick, the ones we use today are made of brass or copper and are in the shape of an L. As a matter of choice we would use two rods and hold one in each hand. Carefully, we would hold the rods with a light grip so they could move without much resistance, but at the same time we made sure it was tight enough to keep them parallel. Then, we would make sure that the handles were held closely to our chests. Our legs would be spread shoulder width apart to avoid any swaying movement. Next, our hands would be tilted so the tips of the rods were at a subtle downward angle.

It is best to begin with some basic trial questions that you can answer yourself such as, "Is my name Shella Hewett?" and "Do I live in Gosport?" The way in which the rods move tells me what they will do for a 'yes' answer. I would then ask some more trial questions to determine how the rods will respond to a 'no' answer.

It is important that the wording of questions is clear and not ambiguous. There are many ways that the rods could move. They could point to the left or the right, swing in opposite directions or swing towards each other and cross. After each question, I always ask spirit to place the rods back in their original position.

When I see a pattern, I can then begin to use the rods on the investigation as I know how to recognise a yes or no answer.

Patience is essential, as it can be a slow process and it takes a lot of practice to use them as they can move with quite some force. I usually keep the sessions short as they require a lot of energy from spirit. If the rods do stop swinging, it means the energy has been lost and that the spirit has drawn back. It is advisable to record the events on a night vision camera so that you can see the answers to the questions you have asked.

Another technique we would use during paranormal investigations, was to see if a 'trigger object' could be moved. A 'trigger object' is an object that is placed in a particular area at a location. We would find a suitable, flat, stable surface and put a piece of white paper on top of it. Then the object is positioned on the paper so that I can carefully draw around it with a marker pen, which is easy for people to see. The idea is to get the spirit to move the 'trigger object'. This is the reason I would outline it so I can see if it moves from its original spot.

Depending upon what object you use, spirit may move it to either get your attention or because the object was of sentimental value to them when they were alive. Typically, I would use an old coin as the 'trigger object' in an endeavour to get a response from spirit although this can be carried out with many different, everyday items. A simple glass or cup are easy to draw around, as is a key or a piece of jewellery such as a ring or a watch. Another commonly used item is a pen and a line can be drawn on a piece of paper, with the pen placed precisely on the line.

If the history of the location is known, it is advisable to bring along something spirit can relate to in the hope that a familiar object will be of interest to them, therefore enticing them to interact. This is the reason I favour using an old coin from the spirits era. To help evoke memories, photographs, picture frames, military medals, tools, bullets and buttons could be used. Some spirits would have enjoyed smoking where they were alive so a pipe, cigar or cigarette would make an apt item.

When trying to interact with spirit children, it is best to reassure them that we are not there to harm them in any way and that we would only like to play a game with them. Understandably, a child spirit may be unsure about communicating with a person they do not know. 'Trigger objects' that are usually well received are toy cars, dolls, teddy bears, crayons, jacks and many other old-fashioned children's playthings. A pretty flower or a chain of daisies might also be appreciated, although the latter would be quite difficult to draw around.

Toys that roll are not recommended, as the slightest breeze or vibration could make them move from their original spot. The same can be said for balls, as they may naturally roll, which make them unstable objects. However, some paranormal investigators choose to use them when trying to attract spirit children because of the playful nature of a child's mind. It seems the temptation of playing with a ball may prove too much for many of them.

Rather than waiting a long time to see if the 'trigger object' moves, we would always set up our night vision camera to record. Most often, objects tend to move when no one is around to observe them so it's important to have a visual record of what took place. Upon recording, I would introduce myself to spirit and respectfully ask them to make their presence known by using their energy to try and move the outlined object. Then we would leave the object for several hours while we continued to investigate the rest of the location. On our return, we would examine the object to see if it was still within the marked outline on the paper.

As I see it, a 'trigger object' gives spirit an opportunity to show they are there. If they recognise something that is dear to them, they can emotionally connect to it which is an encouraging thought. This in turn, means spirit will be more drawn to the object and possibly become more active. That being said, it is rare to capture any movement during these sessions as spirit need an enormous amount of energy to reposition objects.

One piece of equipment that we didn't use on our paranormal investigations is the Ouija board which is also known as a spirit board. This was down to the lead investigators personal preferences. There are different types of Ouija boards but the board usually consists of the letters of the alphabet, the numbers zero to nine and the words 'yes', 'no' and 'goodbye'. It comes with a moveable pointer called a planchette.

In an attempt to contact spirit, people place their right index finger very lightly on the planchette. Then a question is asked and the planchette moves across the board to spell out an answer. Ouija should never be treated as a game or joke, as it is a serious tool for communicating with spirit. Protection should always be sought at the beginning and end of the session, as there can be significant consequences.

Surprisingly, it was on one of our many investigations at the Naval Museum, that Graham and I encountered Elizabeth. While we were taking an unhurried walk around the museum building, we heard an unmistakable knock. It was a knock that made us stop dead in our tracks. Elizabeth was with us. Immediately, I called out to her, hoping she would confirm my suspicion. "Elizabeth, was that you that knocked just now?" Before I could finish asking the question, there was another pronounced knock for yes.

I felt astonished to say the least, as this was the first time Elizabeth had come in visitation outside of our home. To date, it has been the only time. Welcomely, I then asked her, "Are you coming round with us?" She knocked, which led me on to my next question. I had a strong feeling she wasn't alone so I called out, "Have you brought Boy with you?" My intuition had been right as Elizabeth knocked yes in response but then just as quickly, she knocked twice for goodbye.

The session, as short as it was, was recorded with our digital dictaphone so in the early hours of the morning when we returned home, we played the recording back. To our utter amazement, we heard a distinct bark directly after the question

"Have you brought Boy with you?" It appeared he was saying yes in acknowledgement. This was something we hadn't heard while at the museum.

On a number of occasions, we went on paranormal investigations at other locations such as private dwellings, forts and ruins. We would use the same equipment each time but often record noticeably different amounts and types of activity, depending on where we were. Personally, the Naval Museum has been my favourite venue because the actual building itself and its outbuildings all have a magnificent story to tell. I am sad to say they no longer run their paranormal evenings but at least I have been fortunate enough to have experienced many of them.

Chapter 12
By My side

When I began to write this chapter, I received the devastating news that my beloved nan had passed away. My world came crashing down. Nan was ninety-four years of age and the most inspirational person I have had the privilege to have in my life. She was a wonderful role model and helped make me the person I am today.

With emotions running high, it has been difficult to get back into my writing. The day before she died, Nan said to her daughter that she could see a little girl in the living room of her house. When I was told about this, I had a strong feeling the child was Elizabeth. I believe my nan would have known it was Elizabeth too as I had always talked openly about her over the years. Was she providing comfort by letting Nan know it was nearly her time to pass?

Several days later, I made the decision to conduct a spirit box session in the hope that Elizabeth could confirm, that she had been the little girl who had visited my nan. As the session proceeded, I went ahead and asked, "Elizabeth, were you with my nan before she passed over?"

She resoundingly replied, "It was me." I was heartened to discover that Elizabeth had been with my nan, to help her move forward along the path, towards the white light.

Nan. My beautiful nan. We had a very close relationship and I will miss her terribly. Although I know, this is not the end. She has completed one journey and is now beginning her next. I know, as Elizabeth has communicated this to me.

This moves me on to the subject of spirit guides. I feel that everyone has spirit guides and they are assigned to us before we are born until the end of our life. They are positive in nature and are here to guide and support us. We come here to accomplish our life purpose and to learn soul lessons as well as rid ourselves of bad karma.

Spirit guides are here to help us along our path. There are more than one of them and they have an assortment of roles, appearing and interacting in a multitude of ways. One guide will act as our predominant guide, staying with us all of our earthly lifetime but others are around us to help in our daily lives. Frequently, they give us signs, protect us, place opportunities on our path and make every effort to help us make the right choices during our lifetime.

Most people are not consciously aware they have spirit guides or they may not believe in them. Other people have strong connections and greatly depend on them. Each and every one of us has a mission. When we progress into our physical bodies at birth, we usually have no recollection as to why we are here and what our mission is. Fortunately, our guides are with us and will prompt us when the time is right. They have an extensive awareness about our life purpose and will work arduously to make sure we are in the appropriate place at the appropriate time, so that we can achieve our goals during our present lifetime.

Our life path might lead us to grow as a person in certain areas and our spirit guides will try hard to help us, by making sure we get the opportunities to experience these areas. Some people can make this difficult for their guides. It may be that we need to become more considerate, tolerant or helpful to others. The role of a guide is to offer guidance, protection, encouragement and helpfulness.

Even though we all have spirit guides, some independence is still needed as we are in control of our own minds, and are responsible for our own happiness and success. Every now and then, it is relevant for our guides to take initiative and make proposals, as we work together in partnership. It is best to be adaptable to change as sometimes we ask for something, and it doesn't go as planned. Don't forget, there may well be a good reason for this.

I find it astonishing that spirit guides can see many things we cannot and generally know things that we cannot know. Despite this, we should not take it for granted they are always right and we must remind ourselves, they are not here to make our decisions for us. It is important that we learn how to make our own choices so we need to stop ourselves from spontaneously following their advice. We should take a breath and think carefully about what we should choose.

Being able to make contact with our spirit guides should be something that we treasure. This special connection requires patience and much effort. Embrace it as the start of a new relationship that will blossom over time. It can make us feel calm and uplifted, as we know that our guides are always here to help. We must remind ourselves to ask for that help when we need it. I believe it will bring out the best qualities in us and make us a more understanding person.

Nowadays, people have become more open and accepting of the spirit world. This enables us to become closer to our spirit guides so they can make themselves more obviously known. They can share their insight with us as they are more enlightened. Guides want to behold and participate in our spiritual growth.

There are numerous types of spirit guides who work with us throughout our lifetime. Each and every guide have mastered their life here on earth and they have also mastered different levels of the spiritual realm. These guides have their own specific purpose and knowledge, and they present themselves to us in various forms. Often, spirit guides will alter their appearance to suit our line of thought. They do not want to look threatening to us so they choose a form we will find more approachable. I have a natural affinity with animals and children so I understand why Elizabeth projects herself as a child to me.

The first type of spirit guide that I would like to tell you about are our predominant guides. Everyone has at least one main guide, who is always by our side throughout our lifetime. These guides love us unconditionally and they help us follow our life plan, by keeping us on the right path. If we happen to get side-tracked from that path, they will gently nudge us back onto it, providing we are prepared to listen to them. Their role is to give us signs, keep us safe, place opportunities on our path and try to help us make moral choices. It is safe to say, that we are never alone.

A second type of spirit guide are our ancestral guides. These could be spirits from many generations ago that we have never met or more recently passed spirits. Our common bond is that we share the same bloodline and we have a strong spiritual connection with them, which is deep-rooted in us. Consequently, they lovingly watch over and care for us. Their role is to guide, help, protect and heal the living. Ancestral guides can bring wonderful and life-changing messages.

Another type of spirit guide are our past life guides. These guides step forward because of a connection with us in a previous life. They are here to support us through issues we were working on before now and are still working on at the present-time. We all experience troublesome times and our past life guides help us through them. Their role is associated with helping any mental health and emotional difficulties that we may have. Essentially, they want to contribute to the ongoing enrichment of our soul.

A further type of spirit guides is Ascended Masters. These guides' souls have progressed through many lives and incarnations. They have worked through karma, excelled in tests and accomplished their individual reasons for being. As spirit guides they are indispensable because they have accomplished the ultimate goal our souls are aiming for. Their role is to help people who are focused on doing something for the betterment of humanity, the environment or society. Some examples of Ascended Masters are Jesus Christ, Gautama Buddha and Mother Mary.

These spirit guides are the ones that most of us will encounter in our lifetime here on earth but there are also spirits that I call spirit helpers, who are more subtle in their ways. We are not connected to them through a blood tie or from a past life. They have great expertise on whatever it is we are dealing with and choose to help us with our predicament. There are an entire team of spirit helpers working for us and they each take their turn to assist us.

Many people believe there are other guides here to help us, including spirit animals, deities, extra-terrestrials and angels. Each one of us has a different view about spirit guides but we all need guidance, direction and support along the journey that is life. Sometimes, this is beyond our own capabilities and those who are around us. If we allow our guides to step in and help us to understand and learn, then it will be a much smoother path to travel on.

There are many reasons why spirits return to visit us and it very prevalent. From time to time, we might be conscious of a presence around us but at other times, there might be a more obvious sign that someone is wanting to make contact with us. That someone, could be a deceased loved one or our spirit guides trying to make us aware they are with us. Everyone has intuition so we can use our sixth sense to try and access the spirit world. We must open our hearts and minds so we can receive their signals.

A common type of signal from spirit are animals or insects. As spirit use energy to be with us, they direct this energy into them. They present themselves to us as a butterfly, ladybird, dragonfly, bird or various other animals or insects but only for a short amount of time. Typically, they are eye-catching colours so they are easier to spot. To make us take notice of them, they will normally do something that is out of character. It may be that they come into our home, land on our hand or appear right in front of us. Spirits are letting us know they are near and that we are not alone.

It is also very common for spirit to send coins, feathers and other small objects our way. They like to place these in our path where we'll find them. When objects appear out of nowhere, this is known as 'apports' which means gifts from a spirit. In most cases, we keep coins in our purses, wallets and pockets so when we discover one in the strangest of places it grabs our attention. Pennies are often favoured by spirit. Coins can come over and over again, to make us realise that someone is close and wanting to communicate with us. We should focus on our thoughts when finding the coins, as they may contain messages from spirit and have a symbolic meaning.

Often, we will find a white feather that has come out of nowhere. They may be in unusual places like inside our home or in our car. When we receive one, spirit is giving us the comfort that we are watched over and there is a blessing at hand. Sometimes, feathers are left if we are feeling down, in the hope it will give us a lift.

As well as moving objects that don't belong to us, spirit will also move our own belongings. This physical phenomenon is divided into two categories. Firstly, it could be that a treasured picture keeps falling over, even though it's securely put back in its original position. Secondly, objects are moved from one place to another so they disappear and reappear. It seems that spirit see this as a game but it is a game with a meaning. This type of activity is associated with child spirit energies, which explains why Elizabeth uses this method to communicate with me.

Personal items such as a ring, watch or purse may be moved although in my case it's been popcorn kernels, spinners, fridge magnets and the like. People have to be ready to accept this sign and spirit know when that time is. It is not done to frighten us in any way. Spirits are leaving us gifts with a message of love, saying they are with us.

Another method spirit use to try and contact us is through electrical appliances. Countless people have experienced unexplained, flickering lights in their homes or bulbs that blow without justification. These are replaced but when this happens again, an electrician often looks into it, yet a fault cannot be found. Televisions turn on and off or the channels change, radios increase in volume, children's toys start to move around or make noises. The doorbell rings but there is nobody there. A telephone call is made from an unknown number and when answered, there is only static or silence on the other end.

Most of the time, electrical signs mean spirits are with us. There may be some relevance between our line of thought and the activity that has taken place. If we think back carefully, connections could be made. What was on the television when it unexpectedly turned off? Were you thinking of someone when the telephone rang and upon answering, the line was dead?

Scent is a further sign from spirit. They have a way to trigger memories through familiar smells. We often know spirit is near through the sweet scent of flowers, it may be a particular flower they liked, such as roses. People often experience the unmistakable smell of perfume or cigarette/cigar smoke, when no one in close proximity is smoking.

Spirit can also visit and communicate with us through dream visitations, which are much different from ordinary dreams. When we're asleep, our minds are naturally more open to the spirit realm so it's easier for spirit to get through and connect to us. On entering the dream, spirits become visible, looking healthy and vibrant as glowing light surrounds them. They lovingly give us messages by means of words, symbols and scenes that can help guide us in our life. We may even be asked to deliver messages to other people. After spirits have passed on their messages, the serene dream will come to an end. It can take time to make sense of the information that is being given so it's worth jotting it down upon waking.

This type of communication is extremely realistic, detailed and poignant. Above all, dream visitations are very significant. For that reason, it is important that we try to understand what we have been shown and told. These types of dreams will remain in our memory for a long time.

Every now and again, a clock will stop working. This could either be an analogue or a digital clock, spirits are not fussy about which one it is. We should be attentive, as it may show the exact time that someone passed over and this is a sign that spirit is communicating with us. Furthermore, they are making their presence known and want us to remember them.

Number patterns are often shown to us by spirit. People will look at a clock and keep noticing the same time over and over again. Spirit present numbers that hold some significance, such as a time or date a particular person passed away, birth dates, anniversaries and other memorable dates. Repeating numbers such as 11:11, 22:22, 33:33, 44:44 etc. are also seen on clocks. These may be related to numerology, where each number has a valuable meaning to help guide us in life.

In addition, number patterns may be found on number plates and advertisement boards. When we're in the car, we should look around to see if spirits are using this method to contact us. If we do recognise a pattern, it may be a sign that spirits are close by. As always, they bring their love with them.

Music is another sign that spirit is trying to make a connection. One way they do this, is to bring us messages through songs we hear on the radio. I have experienced this through a communication from Elizabeth. We may be thinking about a song that is meaningful to us or spirit and as soon as we turn on the radio, it's playing. Equally, if we are missing someone is spirit, we may hear their favourite song.

Spirits communicate with us through songs from the past as well as through songs we've never heard before. Often, the same song is played as we travel about our daily lives. It may be the first song we listen to in the car, the supermarket or the department store. When we're walking down the road, we may hear it through somebody's window. A film starts on the television, listen to the song that is played at the beginning.

Amazingly, spirits guide us through music. If we constantly hear the same song, it's important to listen to the lyrics to see if they hold a significant message for us. Music stirs up emotions. Sometimes, they are exactly the words we need to hear at that moment in time. Spirit will communicate through songs as the connection is so intense. They want us to know that we are heard and that they are near.

Many times, we have an instinctive 'knowing' about something and this is because our subconscious mind registers thoughts, which our conscious mind is not aware of. Spirits can communicate telepathically and our subconscious may have picked up suggestions from them that lead us to have this strong, intuitive feeling. The spirit world guides us and we should listen to that little voice that lets us know what we need to do. These messages are personal and relevant, and are sent with love.

As well as hearing the voice of a spirit internally, we can also hear them externally. We may hear our name being called but upon looking for someone, no one is there. Therefore, it becomes apparent that spirits are speaking to us in human form. Often, this happens when we are deep in thought so we should try and recall what we were thinking about before our name was called. When this occurs, spirit is attempting to contact us. This is an endearing sign of their presence and is usually experienced when we are in need of solace, reassurance or spiritual guidance.

Unexplained sounds such as footsteps and knocking may also be heard. Having the ability to hear knocking is normal to me, as my main communications with Elizabeth involve knocks in response to the questions that I ask. I am fortunate to be able to hear them, as some people cannot. The volume of the knocks can vary from being faint to crystal clear, depending on how much energy Elizabeth has at the time.

Sometimes, we can feel that spirits are with us through their touch. Although they cannot physically touch us with fingers, they can project their energy onto ours to make us feel like we're being touched. It may feel like cobwebs or actual fingers. A simple gesture such as a brush of our hair, a gentle touch on our cheek or back, a hug or holding our hand are some of the most reassuring forms of contact we may receive. I experienced this, when Boy rested his head on my thigh and similarly, my auntie Jen felt the sensation of Elizabeth stroking her fringe. Often, in moments of sadness and hopelessness we will be lightly touched. This is an affectionate way of expressing that in this world we always have someone watching over us.

Alternatively, a spirit may not touch us but will touch a nearby object. At bedtime, we may notice pressure in bed beside us, as if someone is in the process of laying down. Or we could be sat on the settee having a quiet moment, when it feels like someone is sitting next to us. We shouldn't feel frightened or threatened by these visits, as spirits only want to be close to us.

There are times, when we have this strange feeling that we're not alone even though we are alone. Intuitively, we can sense a spirit near us although we cannot see or hear them. It may feel like someone is standing right behind us but on turning around, no one is there. A Spirit is letting us know that it is with us and that we are watched over and loved.

Often, people feel a cold breeze as if someone has walked past them. The temperature of the room might suddenly drop, even though all the windows and doors are shut. Goosebumps appear on our arms as the chill intensifies. This unexplained current of air affects us in such a way, that we know a spirit is present.

Heat can also affect us, as much as the cold. Usually, this warm feeling stays with us for a long time after we first experience it. We may feel deeply connected to a spirit. This communication is one of comfort and tenderness.

Seeing a full apparition is one of the spiritual signs that we are least likely to encounter. I believe this to be the case because Elizabeth has never shown herself to me. It takes an enormous amount of energy for spirit to be able to manifest but I don't feel this is the reason why I haven't seen her. I say this, as Graham has witnessed a vision of Elizabeth already.

Casually, I was making my way towards the living room from the kitchen. As I passed the dining room door, Graham distinctly saw a young girl about a step behind me. Appearing as a solid human form, her smiling face was above my right shoulder. Graham looked at her in amazement and realised it must be Elizabeth. For one brief instant, he averted his eyes but on second glance, she had disappeared from sight.

As I see it, I would rather not be able to see a spirit because I would find it somewhat overwhelming, and I feel that Elizabeth knows this. Consequently, she interacts with me using methods that she feels I can cope with. In turn, I am always comfortable with how Elizabeth approaches me. I wouldn't change a single thing about her.

In addition to a solid human form, apparitions can materialise as either misty or transparent. For a fleeting moment, some people may see an unexplained shadow from the corner of their eye. Brightly coloured, spherical shapes called orbs are also often spotted. Sometimes, they cannot be seen with the naked eye but commonly show up in photographs. There may be glowing, white lights that twinkle or dart across the room. Spirits can take on all of these different forms. They direct our attention and thoughts towards them, to make us aware they are near.

Sensing a spirit's presence by sight, smell, hearing and touch helps us keep in mind they still exist. These visits bring messages of love, hope and inspiration and can symbolise something of great importance. If spirits have not presented themselves to us, we can reach out to them instead. People everywhere can access the spirit realm but it involves a lot of practice, patience and a focused mind.

Chapter 13
Elizabeth

Elizabeth. This is her story to tell. Over the past twelve years, I have kept detailed records about the phenomena that had taken place. These individual accounts were then tucked away in different drawers and units. Little did I know, I would ever put them to good use.

I began thinking about writing a book some years ago now and after piecing all the paperwork together, I managed to complete the first chapter. Strangely enough, it went missing from the place I had always left it. For that reason, the idea of continuing to write was put on hold until one day, I came across the lost chapter in a completely different area of my house. It was on the floor, under the first-floor stairs. What ceased to amaze me was that I had been meaning to start the book again so I took this as a sign to push forward with my writing.

Meticulously, I reread the pages and decided to stick with what I had written, only changing a few words here and there.

This time, I was determined to record all of the paranormal events that I had encountered. If I was writing and had a case of writers block, I would frequently ask Elizabeth for guidance, and when asked, she would encourage and reassure me that the book would get published and be a success. Subsequently, this always gave me the incentive to keep going. After all, I was writing the book about, and for her.

My belief is that Elizabeth is here to guide me in life, as well as many other reasons and she has guided me to write, which would help me grow as a person. Each time I had written up my notes, I would throw the tatty, old pieces of paper away knowing they were now part of a book. I'm just so thankful that I kept all of these notes, otherwise I wouldn't have been able to share my experiences with other people. As I see it, there are various books, films and television programmes about negative spirits but not so many about positive spirits, so I feel it is important to draw special attention to Elizabeth.

Mia has recently started university and is living in student accommodation. Her long-time friend Caitlin, is studying the same degree course and shares a room with her. Before moving in together, they had a disagreement about whether pineapple should be a topping on pizza. Mia was adamant that pineapple on pizza should not go together and that it made an awful combination, whilst Caitlin felt they complimented each other. To settle the argument, Mia decided on a plan of action. She would use the spirit box to ask Elizabeth a question.

When Mia arrived home later that evening, she told me about her conversation and asked me to set up the spirit box. As we were about to start the session, Mia said she wanted me to speak to Elizabeth because she thought that we would get a better response if I communicated with her. I lit a candle and switched on the device, before saying some words of protection. The session was opened.

Feeling confident that Elizabeth would be with me, I called out clearly

"Elizabeth, are you here?" In next to no time, her voice came through. I couldn't quite understand what she was trying to say but at least I knew she was near. It wasn't long, before I asked the all-important question that I hoped would settle Mia and Caitlin's argument. "Elizabeth, I hope you can answer this question, does pineapple belong on pizza?" A few seconds past before she replied a definite "No." I was amazed at how quickly Elizabeth had responded. It appeared that Mia's point of view was correct. Keeping the session short, I went on to say, "Thank you Elizabeth for answering the question," and then I said, "Goodbye."

The next day, Mia was more than happy to let Caitlin know the outcome. Elizabeth had provided the definitive answer. Mia had even recorded the session as proof that it took place. It seems that a spirit is more than willing to assist us in answering less meaningful questions, as well as the more important ones in life.

I often think about how easy it was for me to first communicate with Elizabeth.

What made it straightforward, is the fact that she was the one who made the initial contact. Admittedly, I had been very fortunate in this respect because this is not always the case for everyone. I recognised the sign she was giving me so I was then able to respond, and make that spiritual connection.

The fact that a soul can call forth in spirit, is an astonishing revelation in itself. It seems that spirits are attracted to people who can sense them more clearly and they know exactly who that is. Spirits convey themselves through the psychic senses and as I'm a highly sensitive person, it enables me to sense Elizabeth's energy much more consciously. Furthermore, it makes it easier for her to connect with me.

I strongly believe I have a spiritual gift, which is helping me to fulfil my life's purpose. This gift deepens and enriches me as a human being. Usually, I know how other people are feeling, merely by looking at them and I find that their moods can rub off on me, and affect how I feel. Animals are often drawn to me without any encouragement and if I'm able to place my hand on them, I can normally pick up on their emotional state.

Being intuitive is a part of my make-up, as much as I am honest and kind-hearted. Over the course of time, I realised that I had this natural ability and in turn, this has allowed Elizabeth to bring me more frequent and stronger messages. When I communicate with her, I do it in a positive and effective way which supports me on the path ahead. I'm aware that Elizabeth knows me inside out, my every thought and feeling. I don't really have to tell her out loud, for she has the ability to understand what is in my mind without words.

Coming into contact with a child spirit is rare because of the innocence surrounding their spirit at the time of death. If they do present themselves to us, we should consider ourselves very privileged that we've been chosen. Like Elizabeth, child spirits are lively souls who enjoy playing games and are full of mischief. They are simply trying to attract our attention so they can make that initial connection with us.

Elizabeth was extremely active when she first came to me, as our energies were strongly connected. We also had a heartfelt, emotional bond from the very beginning. This is usual where child spirits are concerned. Often, they seek those who remind them of someone in their previous life. They identify easiest with the people who are prepared to listen to them and I am one such person.

Most of the time, child spirits are drawn to women who are mothers. This is especially the case, if they see a specific woman who reminds them of their own mother from their earthly life. It may be that the woman has a similar appearance to the mother or has qualities in common with her. Sometimes, it is a combination of both of these characteristics.

Child spirits are also attracted to our family dynamics because they are interested in the roles of the family members, and how they relate to one another. Perhaps Elizabeth relates to me because I have a husband, a daughter and a son, which is the same as her family unit. The earliest indication, was when she referred to Graham and me as 'Mum and Dad' by using the fridge magnets. This then proceeded with further communications by this method that were along the same lines. When I've asked Elizabeth verbally if she thinks of us as her mum and dad, she has knocked once for yes. Even though I feel happy about this, a part of me feels sad because I cannot physically interact with her like a loving mother should.

We often regard a mother's love as the most profound type of love. Mothers offer unconditional love, which doesn't depend on the circumstances of the child. I know I've not been the one who taught Elizabeth to walk, talk or smile. What's more, I have not comforted her in my arms or embraced her when she wanted to show her love. Also, I have not had sleepless nights taking care of Elizabeth when she was unwell. I may not have created Elizabeth or known entirely what she has gone through but I have snippets of information that have helped me to create pictures in my mind.

Occasionally, I have to remind myself that Elizabeth is only a child because she guides me in life, rather than the other way round. It's almost like the roles should be reversed, as she is like a mother to me. Thankfully, Elizabeth gives me a sense of direction and sometimes redirection, which keeps me on the right path. What seven-year-old child on this Earth plane could possibly have such knowledge and capability?

People have often asked me if I have researched the history of my house. This is something I have never got round to doing but I do intend to in the near future. I understand it is a fairly straightforward process to trace the former occupants of a house, with the aid of government records and archive material. To be able to do this, I would have to find out Elizabeth's surname, as I haven't questioned it before. The reason I haven't asked her, is because I've never needed to know. Elizabeth, is quite simply Elizabeth to me.

Our relationship commenced from a place of love and this has grown as time goes by. It is one of the purest bonds there is and Elizabeth and I will always share this unique bond, no matter how far apart we may be. She knows all about me, even hidden secrets in the depths of my heart. From the embarking of our time together until the end of our time together, Elizabeth can always depend on me. When life gets difficult and I feel all alone, I remember that I mean the world to her and that she calls me Mum. Elizabeth flies free and I will always love her but this is only the beginning.